The Lunch

The Bench

Living A Meaningful Life

by
Brian Hunter

*Published by
Wizard Way
Rainbow Wisdom
Ireland*

Copyright © 2021 Brian Hunter

All rights reserved.
No part of this publication may be reproduced, stored in a retrieval system, or transmitted, in any form or by any means, electronic, mechanical, photocopying, recording or otherwise without the prior permission of *Rainbow Wisdom*

This book is sold subject to the condition that it shall not, by way of trade or otherwise, be lent, re-sold, hired out, or otherwise circulated without the publisher's prior consent in any form of binding or cover other than that in which it is published and without a similar condition including this condition being imposed on the subsequent purchaser.
Names have been modified in the book to protect the identities of certain individuals. Others are included with full permission. While others are too strongly recognized by universal consciousness to be concealed.

ISBN: 9798766395089

DEDICATION

This book is dedicated to all those with the courage to do the right thing, and to those who give to others in order to create a better future.

CONTENTS

1	The Bench	7
2	The Grumpy Old Man	41
3	The Silent Bully...........................	67
4	The Love Story ….............……..	99
	Acknowledgments.............………...	139
	About The Author…………..........	140
	Also, by Brian Hunter……….……...	141
	Living A Meaningful Life Series Synopsis...	145

CHAPTER ONE

The Bench

I discovered the bench for the first time when I was maybe nine years old, or perhaps younger. I suppose it had always been there before that, but when you are a kid, you tend not to really notice things unless they are directly relevant to you. We lived near a park, and I used to ride my snazzy blue and red bicycle to the park when I was bored, or when I was trying to meet up with friends. The park was a place where you could see all different kinds of people. Sometimes there would be adults walking a dog, young kids playing kickball in the grass, older kids hanging out with their bikes strewn about on the grass, teenagers taking girls there on dates, and older people sitting on the bench watching it all.

I specifically remember the old lady who always used to sit there on the park bench passing time. I was kind of intrigued with her for some reason, and often wondered about her life and what an amazing life she must have lived based upon all the legends and rumors I had heard. Her name was Mrs. Carlisle, but for some reason my mom and some of the parents in town called her "Momma B." All I knew was that she had been a very important person in town, even legendary.

I guess her husband had died some years ago, and she had donated the bench in his memory because they always used to sit there together. It originally had a plaque on it that said his name, but at some point the plaque was scraped off by someone, or it fell off. Nobody ever knew if it was some kid who did it, or like my mom said, there was a rumor that Mrs. Carlisle herself might have removed it for some reason. Eventually though, the old lady seemed to be there less and less until she wasn't seen there at all anymore. I guess it was kind of considered to be her bench, but once she wasn't sitting there all the time, all the kids took it over as their own.

I remember the bench so well because it was pretty much the heart of the park, and the park was pretty much the heart of the town, other than the high school. At the time, when I was a young kid, the bench looked really big, new, shiny, and was the newest and nicest thing in the park. It sat with trees in back of it providing shade, and a walkway in front of it so you could see everyone and everything, and everyone could see you. There was a great view of the large expanse of grass in front of you with a random spattering of maple and oak trees, along with a few very large pine trees that would drop these really cool pine cones.

The park was beautiful, but a beauty that was only noticed and appreciated more with age. The lush grass was always mowed, and yet nobody ever saw anyone mowing it. It was one of those magical things that happened when you are a child, when you do not realize the work and consequences behind causing such "magical" things to happen.

Also unrealized as a child was the significance the park bench would play in my life. When we are young we think within the moment only. We think in narrow moments of time, usually in the present. I had no idea how much broader my view of life would become as I learned and grew. I also had no idea of the significance the park, and that bench specifically, would play in everyone's lives.

Some of my best memories as a child were playing with friends in that park. We would often use the park bench as a meeting place to throw down our bicycles and see who else was there. Depending on how many of us showed up, we would play games, or just hang out together. If we were lucky, someone would have brought a ball of some sort. I can remember many spontaneous kickball games starting up. Other times it might be whiffle ball. Sometimes it was a football. We would play in the grass, with kids tackling each other, which would sometimes turn into a wrestling match. If girls started watching, the competition would all of a sudden go from a fun and leisure scale of 3, all the way up to a dead-serious scale of 10 death match. The best part of the whole thing was that you never knew what would happen that day. It was always so spontaneous. All you knew was that you needed to show up and be ready for anything.

Sometimes on hot summer days, the ice cream truck would come to the park and everyone would run to the street and try to be the first in line to buy an ice cream treat of some sort. Then the race would be to see who could run from the ice cream truck to the bench, for a guaranteed prime place to sit and enjoy the ice cream. How many kids can sit on one park bench? A LOT. You could cram a half dozen kids on the bench seat, but then also one each on the ends of the bench. Others could lean against the back. Everyone else would end up on the grass or sitting on their bikes.

There was a communal feeling amongst the younger kids. We may have come from separate families, but while at the park we were all one family, brothers and sisters. We were competitive at our games, but when it came down to it, we always looked out for one another. If one kid got hurt, we would run over to him while he was writhing in pain on the grass, and there would be as many as ten kids asking him at the same time if he was alright. If the kid seemed really hurt and couldn't stop crying, a few of us would help him up and walk him all the way back to his house, while another kid walked his bicycle home for him, and then others would follow in support.

I remember seeing startled looks on the faces of moms who would receive a special delivery of their wounded child by numerous other children, all trying to explain in different ways all at once how their child got injured. I didn't think of it back then, but I imagine as a parent it must have been a warm comforting feeling to see so many other kids going out of their way to help and make sure their injured friend got back home safely.

When I think of adult life today and what much of our society has turned into, I wonder why our world could not be like that group of kids, helping each other, and carrying the full weight of anyone who just couldn't cope with life at a particular moment. The innocence of youth can at times be an inspiration of how we should all be in the present as adults, and not just of how we were in the past while growing up.

Not all days were sunny and full of friends and fun. There were some days I would go to the park and nobody was there. Unfortunately for me, those were usually the days that I really needed some companionship. I may have gotten yelled at by my mother or stepfather, or stood up by a friend who promised to do something with me that day, or maybe I was just feeling sad and lonely for one reason or another.

On days when I was feeling down, misunderstood, or excluded, and found myself totally alone at the park, I would sit on the park bench and contemplate life. I would wonder why some people have to be mean, or why they don't care about my feelings, or why nobody truly listens. Looking back, it was not necessarily negative life events that hurt me the most. Usually what hurt me the most was when other people didn't care enough to take the time to listen and try to understand me on deeper levels. A person can handle bad life events if they have loving support from others, but when a person is seemingly left, abandoned, and forgotten, it can become impossible to deal with any life situation at all, never mind a bad one.

I would sit on that bench and realize that perhaps much of my life would include those lonely moments, and that I best become very comfortable with that. And so I did. I don't know how old I was exactly, but there came a point when sometimes I would actually HOPE nobody was at the park, so that I could sit there alone in peace to think.

I had become comfortable with solitary moments of reflection. I realized that if I became comfortable with myself, being alone, and only relied upon myself, that maybe I would not be let down or disappointed by others. I believe this was the moment in my life when I started to become the very independent person I am today.

It was on just such a lonely day as a young teenager, when I was sitting on the bench with nobody else in sight, and my entire world changed. I had been having increasing problems dealing with my parents, and as usual had escaped my home to sit at the park where I could at least have some peace. It was kind of a cold gloomy day, so I was not surprised to not see anyone else at the park.

I was deep in thought as usual, contemplating life, when all of a sudden my moment of solitary peace and loneliness was interrupted. From out of nowhere this girl was magically standing in front of me and said,

"Is it okay if I sit here too?"

I, in a very uninviting cold way said, "Sure, I guess so."

She immediately acted upon my frigid and somewhat rude acceptance, and had a seat on the opposite end of the bench.

I knew who she was. She was in my grade at school, but we never talked, so I didn't really know her that well. She lived at the opposite side of the park from me, so while I had seen her at the park before with her own friends, I never saw her on my neighborhood street where most of my friends lived.

She was a sweet and gorgeous girl, and I am not sure how or why I was so stupid as to not have any interest in recognizing the opportunity to pursue her in a meaningful way. By the way I had just acknowledged her, you would think I had zero interest in her. Lucky for me, she did not take any offense or get discouraged by my initial reaction to her.

She started the conversation by saying that she had seen me sitting here often alone, and wanted to know whether it was because I was sad, or because I liked being alone. I answered by saying,

"Both and neither."

She laughed and said that made complete sense to her. Looking back, I believe it was that response by her that immediately sold me on her. I think I liked her from that moment on. If she was fishing, she had easily caught this pathetic fish, using only that one response of agreeing with my nonsensical sense of humor and self-pity, mixed with factual reality.

We started talking, and talking, and talking. We must have sat there for many hours talking that first day. It turned out that she was very similar to me in that she had issues with her parents, and she had become more independent from her childhood friends. While she didn't spend much time mindlessly sitting on the park bench like myself, she DID spend lots of time aimlessly walking around the outskirts of the park near the trees and flowering bushes.

Perhaps I just never noticed before?

How could I not notice?

Was I that lost within my own self and inner angst?

"Yes," is the answer.

We started meeting at the park almost every day, whether it be after school, or on weekends. I considered her my best friend. Yes, she was a GIRL, yes I was physically attracted to her, BUT perhaps I was just too intimidated to turn it into a "romantic relationship." I simply loved being with her, talking with her, and having that emotional support of someone I considered very close to me. I think it was really the fact she UNDERSTOOD me. But I think she was ready for more than just "friends."

One day while we were sitting on the bench talking, she said to me

"How come you don't ask me to be your girlfriend?"

I was taken off guard by the question, and at the same time I felt bad, because I was afraid she was feeling rejected by me, and I empathized with that, if that makes any sense. I responded to her by saying,

"I ALREADY consider you my girlfriend."

She replied, "Yeah, but you never asked."

There was an awkward silence. I wasn't sure what to do. I felt bad that she was feeling neglected by me in some way. I truly cared about her as sort of a girlfriend already anyway.

Then, being the very stupid boy I was, I said to her,

"What will be the difference if you are my girlfriend?"

How romantic of me, yes? Yes, stupid I know. However, she did not take offense and was ready. She responded,

"Well, as your girlfriend we can hold hands and know that we are only interested in each other."

I thought about that for a moment and absolutely loved the implications of that. So I said,

"Yes, okay."

"Yes, okay what?" She replied.

"You can be my girlfriend."

She sighed in frustration, and I knew I had screwed something up. I realized my mistake and said to her,

"But I need to ask you first." I then got all dramatic, partly to be funny about it since this entire conversation was already a mess, and I got up from the bench, walked to the other end where she was sitting, and I got down on one knee in front of her. I said,

"Will you please be my girlfriend?" I was expecting an immediate "yes" answer and an end to all of this nonsense. I didn't get it. Instead, she said

"Why should I be your girlfriend?" Without even thinking, I said immediately and naturally,

"Because you are already my best friend, and I love being with you."

I saw her face change, except this time to something nice. She said,

"Yes, I will be your girlfriend."

I smiled, and she smiled, and then I reached out for her hand as if to help her stand up off the bench. But instead of releasing her hand after she stood up, I kept a hold of her hand. We then walked around the park hand in hand.

It was official. I had my first girlfriend.

As I was enjoying my early teenage years with my first official girlfriend, whom I perceived as the eternal love of my life, I became fixated on that relationship as if it were the only thing of importance in my life. I wanted to spend all of my time with her. She was all I thought about while at home, while at school, and while any place else. I looked forward to our time after school and on weekends. Much of our time together was at the park, aimlessly walking around or sitting on the bench talking about nothing and everything. But one day would be more memorable than others.

It started off as a beautiful warm Saturday morning, and we were set to meet up at the park for a full "date day." Saturday was our favorite day because it was the one day that we could be together all day. I was excited and arrived at the bench first. I had a special surprise for my girl. I had managed to buy this nice little necklace to give her. It didn't cost much money, but you wouldn't think so by all the effort and care I put into choosing just the right one, which I got from a mail-order outlet. It was the first jewelry gift I had ever given anyone, including my girl. I'm pretty sure I was more excited to give it to her than she would be receiving it, but that's okay.

As I sat on the park bench waiting for her, I finally saw her walking along the walkway toward me. She was wearing a dress I had never seen before. I could tell it was new, and part of me wondered what the special occasion was that would cause her to wear such a beautiful new outfit, as we usually went very informal. Perhaps somehow we both knew deep down inside that it would be a special day.

She walked up to me smiling, and sat down on the bench next to me. There was no hug or kiss because we had not done that yet. For us, holding hands was a really big deal and felt very intimate and intense just doing that. So, she put her hand on mine when she sat down, and I grabbed her hand to hold it. Her hands always felt so soft and caused me to feel things I didn't understand that well. We talked a bit about random everythings and nothings just like always, until we decided to get up and walk around the park.

We walked along the outer edge of the park holding hands while I tried to decide when to give her the necklace. Finally, we reached this nice spot with some flowering bushes amongst the trees. I stopped and told her that I had something for her. She seemed confused and intrigued. I reached into my pocket and took out the necklace, which was by this time a tangled mess. I quickly realized this was going to be the most botched romantic presentation in history. She saw it and immediately got all excited as if to help me through the botched presentation.

Being a clever boy, I told her that the necklace was like our lives. It was a tangled mess, but that I would untangle it for her until it became a thing of beauty, just like her. Okay, maybe it was corny. But clever for a young teenager. Even more clever was that somehow I was able to untangle the huge mess in a short amount of time. I tried to hide my own surprise of salvaging the situation through a lucky miracle, and instead presented it as my sheer brilliance and talent for untangling necklaces.

I made a proper presentation to her and she asked if I would help her put it on. UGH. You mean untangling the huge mess was not enough??? The struggle was not over yet?? I said, "Okay," and I sort of stood there like an idiot not sure what to do next. Then I realized how stupid I was being, and what she was up to with her request. This was her excuse to allow me to sort of put my arms around her as I placed the necklace around her neck. She turned around so I could struggle with the clasp, which I knew nothing about. Fortunately, I was still clever enough to figure that one out as well. The necklace was on, and she seemed delighted. I could tell her delight because instead of just grabbing my hand as usual, she caressed my lower arm and hand first, before grabbing it. This was a first. This was when I realized that giving girls jewelry had its benefits.

However, during all the necklace drama I failed to notice that clouds had quickly come out of nowhere, and this perfect sunny day looked like it was going to turn into rain. Sure enough it started to sprinkle, and then it started to rain. We ran under some trees for shelter and I asked her if she wanted to go home. Her reply was that if a tangled necklace could not stop us, then neither should a little rain. She said that the rain was like our lives, and that we could choose to run from the rain, or we could choose to dance in the rain. I smiled and laughed at how much more clever she was than me. Before I could make the first move, she grabbed my hand and pulled me out into the rain.

And yes, we then danced in the rain. It was with inhibited hesitation at first, but then we both became so soaked that it no longer mattered. At that point we both danced together in the rain as if there were no tomorrow. I can't even tell you how long this went on for because time did not exist in that moment. We just danced, ran, frolicked, and danced some more. Eventually we somehow ended up back near the park bench. By this time, the sun was peeking through the clouds again, and there was a rainbow amongst the light rain still falling. We both sat down on the park bench at the same time as if choreographed. We sat very close and were both looking at the rainbow. But then all of a sudden, we both turned to each other at the same time. And it happened.

We looked at each other, both totally soaking wet, and both totally lost in the moment, with time not existing. Her face met my face and we kissed for the very first time. It was a very light, romantic, but awkward kiss at first. But then we gently went in for seconds (my second kiss?) (or part of the first kiss?) and we kissed like we meant it this time. Words cannot adequately describe the feeling of an amazing genuine loving first kiss between two young new lovers, but maybe this makes it that much more magical. We kissed several more times as we sat on the park bench soaking wet looking at the rainbow.

I might have preferred to think that life could be frozen in that moment of perfection, but it must not have because eventually I was back home lying in bed that night, in heaven thinking about what an amazing day I just had. My first kiss.

I thought my life could not get much better. Despite any issues with my parents, school, or anything else, I was happy with life, and felt the good times would never end as long as I had her. I guess without realizing it, I had gone from a very solitary independent person, to someone who was COMPLETELY dependent on the love, support, and companionship of another. Weird how that can happen.

But after a while, I felt some changes in her behavior and feelings. She started saying she was too busy to meet all the time anymore. She started sharing a little bit less of herself when we were together. It all started to feel more distant, but it happened gradually enough that I was not totally alarmed about it. Anyone could have seen it coming, except me of course. Everyone knows what comes next. A first love is just that. It's a FIRST love. Meaning, there will be more after that. Meaning, the first one ends at some point.

It was another nice sunny day on a Saturday morning, and we were set to meet at the park as usual. I arrived first and sat on the bench waiting for her. She was already about ten minutes late when I saw her walking up the pathway toward me. She had a gentle beauty to her, while also having a sense of gloom on her face. She only wore jeans and a jacket instead of one of her usual bright skirts or dresses. Her hair was left free and long instead of primping and styling as she usually did it. She basically looked the way people look when they are bringing bad news.

She sat down on the bench, but left a bit of space between us. She said nothing at first. I asked her if she was okay. She said she was doing good. I asked her how she can be doing good when she doesn't look like she is doing good. She ignored my question. Instead, she asked me if I knew a certain boy in school. I said I had heard of him but wasn't friends with him. She paused and said,

"Well me and him have been spending lots of time together at school."

I started to become upset deep inside because I knew what this was. I managed to stammer out the words "Okay well that's nice."

She then said, "We decided to be together."

I responded, "WE? You mean you and me? Because WE are WE."

She felt I was becoming defensive and angry.

She was wrong.

I was not defensive OR angry.

I was extremely HURT.

More like mortally wounded.

She said, "We, meaning me and him."

I said, "So you don't want me anymore."

Then I started to cry a little, while desperately trying to not cry a lot. How could it get worse? It was bad enough I was destroyed inside, but now I had to be humiliated by crying in front of someone, especially her. All I could do was choke out the word "Okay." I then spent all my energy on trying to hold all my crying inside. I wiped my eyes and nose with my hand and once again said,

"Okay."

She asked if I was okay. I said,

"No, but I'm fine." I said to her, "You are okay, so I guess that's all that matters."

I then saw pity in her eyes as she was watching me sniveling, crying, with snot starting to leak out my nose.

I felt so embarrassed at this point, I just wanted it to be over.

I told her she could go and it's okay.

She hesitated, acting like she was about to say something. But she stopped and just stood up. She looked at me, dropped her head, and looked at the ground.

Then she just walked away.

She walked away from me.

She left me.

There.

Alone.

Walked away from me.

I needed to have a volcano eruption of emotion, but wanted her far enough away and out of sight first.

After I felt she was totally gone and away from the park, I erupted into the most incredible painful crying fit I think I ever had.

I just sat on the bench and sobbed like my life had ended, and the world with it. The pain was so intense I felt everything breaking inside me. I think I died inside. I could barely breathe from the crying, and that is when I started to calm down and become silent. All that was left were some leftover random tears and a deep hollow feeling inside me.

I was destroyed.

I was nothing inside.

I was dead.

I sat on that bench motionless and just stared out at nothing.

I was back to being alone again, but far worse than before.

After the breakup, I became very silent. I went to school and focused on my school work, then I would go immediately home, where I would stay in my bedroom doing homework, or nothing at all. This went on for a few weeks. I had lost all interest in friends, activities, and life in general. But as if that was not bad enough, I started having more problems with my parents.

I am not sure if me being home more often was causing the problem, or if it was something else, but it just felt as if my parents were hating on me more, no matter how much I tried to avoid them. I think they wanted me to get a job, get involved in a school sport, or go do something. They talked about wanting me to "do what normal kids do." Of course, inside I was screaming back at them,

"I AM NOT NORMAL. WHAT EVEN IS THAT?"

I have since realized that nobody is normal. Thus, to this day I still have no idea what they were talking about. There is no normal. Kids ARE who they ARE. Let people be who they ARE. Let people be who they want to be. Let them be what and who they feel they are. Stop telling people that what they are is not okay. Stop telling people they need to be "normal."

Anyway, the tensions only continued to increase. My despair over the breakup was replaced by my anger and frustration over dealing with my parents. I started going to the park again just as a way of escaping the torture within my home. I even started doing some of my homework at the park. I would sit on the bench and read my book assignments. Sometimes other friends from school would show up at the park and I would socialize a bit. I was finally able and willing to be social and communicative again at least. I might have been depressed, but at least I was part of the living world again.

Much to my own surprise, I had become fairly comfortable with life again, and especially being alone at the park. I was still broken deep inside, but it really is true when they say time heals. I was not that upset about the breakup anymore. She had ended up breaking up with her new boyfriend anyway. We were all getting older, and some of us were changing more than others. She had changed a lot and was no longer the same person I had fallen in love with. This helped my healing a lot. Somehow having her no longer being a person I wanted to be with fixed it for me.

I got into a really nice routine of always going to the park, doing some of my homework, and always socializing with anyone from school who might show up. Sometimes I would just sit motionless and think. It was not in a sad though. It was just sitting on the bench and thinking about life, thinking about the future, and I was starting to develop an appreciation for the familiar nature that had surrounded me since I was a small child. The park had become more of a home to me than my actual home with my parents.

It turned out that I was not the only kid having issues with their parents. There was another kid from school who also started showing up to the park more often. I knew him from school, but I didn't really know him because we were from different friend groups. I was kind of a strait-laced student who always followed the rules and did my homework. He was a kid known for his trips to the principal's office. I had fully assumed that maybe he was a "problem child" into bad things and should be avoided. My ignorant assumptions had deceived me.

After hesitantly talking with him on and off at the park for a while, I began to feel he was a really cool guy. He seemed kind, intelligent, and willing to listen. How could he be a "bad kid?" It was confusing to me. I guess you could say we gradually and naturally became friends. It helped that we had one major thing in common. We both had major issues at home. While my parents seemingly hated me and enjoyed torturing me, at least my parents never hit me and always made sure I had everything I needed. However, it was not like that for my new friend. His parents were outright abusive. His mother was a drunk or something, and his father was very violent and would even hit him sometimes. I couldn't understand why his father would hit someone that seemed like a really good kid.

It started to become clear to me that he was only getting into trouble at school because he was tired of everyone's bullshit, and would often talk back to teachers or other kids who gave him a hard time. He was actually very smart and if he studied before a test, he would get an A.

To make a long story a little shorter, he became my best friend at this particular school. We ended up hanging out at the park every day. I think I was a good influence on him because he started doing his homework with me. His grades started to improve, and he got into trouble less at school. There were also times that I let him stay over at my house when his parents were out of control. My parents seemed to like him okay, and I think they were relieved I had a friend to do things with, so they wanted to encourage the friendship.

For the first time since being with my girlfriend, I was laughing again. My friend and I would go for pizza, ice cream, and hang out with other friends. I introduced him to my friend group, and he introduced me to his friend group. It was great for both of us to meet other kids different than those we would normally hang out with. Eventually, there were times when my friend group and his friend group would all be at the park at the same time. We all started hanging out together sometimes. It was really fun.

It was a good time of life for me. I had zero interest in chasing girls or having another relationship that would end painfully. Instead, I preferred hanging out with all my friends, and especially my best friend who always made me laugh without me having to always entertain him or others like I would have to do with girls.

The summer during this phase of my life was probably the best summer I ever had. We were all older teenagers by now, and had permission to stay out after dark. All of us would meet at the park and hang out until late at night. Have you ever in your life had a group of friends that made you feel so incredibly happy and at ease that you considered them your family? All of my friends that summer were my family. We were together every day, horsed around together, laughed together, showed support for each other when needed, and always had each other's back. I considered my home (where my parents lived) to just be a place where I ate and slept. I had very little interaction with my parents, and that seemed to work for me and them. So be it. My family were my friends at the park. It was a coming-of-age time for some of us, and a few of my friends got their first serious girlfriend during this time. There were times when a friend with his girlfriend might "disappear" for a few minutes. Where did they go I wonder? Well, we would all certainly give them a hard time when they would come back, because we all knew what they were doing in private, and they were guilty as charged even if it turned out they were innocent.

For me, I still had zero interest in finding a new girlfriend. Between my best friend and my larger friend group at the park, I was happier than I had ever been. Why would I change that? So I didn't. However, time has a way of passing, and eventually the summer ended and we were all going back to high school. Although I was sad for my perfect summer at the park to end, I was hoping that maybe school would expand my social life by allowing me to meet more people who were not from my immediate neighborhood. Plus, me and all my friends could still meet at the park after school. I had planned to continue doing my homework at the park bench, and at the very least hanging out with my best friend who would continue to do the same.

But that was not to be. After school, I started to find myself COMPLETELY ALONE at the park again. Everyone seemed to have vanished and gone deeply into their "school life," which did not include the park apparently. However, I had assumed my best friend would still be with me. After all, I was his critically important key to escaping his horrible parents and home life. What would he do without me? Certainly, he would not vanish as well?

But he did. He vanished. He vanished without a word to me. It left me really confused. I know we had not had a fight about anything. I knew he was still at school and seemed really happy. So what was wrong? Why didn't he want to be my friend anymore? Why is it that the people I open up to the most, become the closest to, and trust the most, are always the people who abandon me? I kept reminding myself that we were not in any kind of romantic relationship or anything, so I shouldn't get too dramatic. He had every right to stop hanging out with me. It's not like he was obligated. But still.

It took a few weeks before I finally got all my answers. I was sitting at the park alone when I saw off in the distance him walking with some girl. I started watching them and noticed them laughing and touching each other and stuff. Obviously, he had a girlfriend now. I had been replaced. Even worse, he never even told me. He just left me without any word or warning. Is that what friends do? They hang out with you until someone more interesting and better comes along?

It's not like I cried or anything, but to be honest I was really depressed and let down by it. I think what hurt me most is that he didn't even tell me himself. Maybe if he had explained he had a girlfriend now and couldn't hang out very often, I would have been okay with that. But he didn't want to share his personal life with me anymore. That is what hurt.

When people do this to you, it makes you question if there is something wrong with you. You wonder if maybe you are not that great or interesting of a person. Or maybe people are just using you. It makes you feel used up and thrown away.

I must be such complete worthless garbage, that my best friend did not even find me worthwhile to share that he had a girlfriend and was in love.

Was he lying to me all along when he was sharing his personal life with me?

Or was I just no longer worthwhile because the girl was better?

Ridiculous questions, I know.

Pointless questions. But we ask them anyway, don't we.

Chalk up my best friend experience as another disappointment in life. Maybe I can't have a girlfriend AND I ALSO cannot have a best friend. I do not want the pain of abandonment. I noticed my happiest moments in life were when I was with others, BUT my most stable moments in life were when I was alone and independent. Maybe it's better to be alone and stable?

That is the thought I kept in my head for quite a while as I sat on the park bench alone, once again, for quite a while. I sat there doing my homework, contemplating life, and thinking nothing at all. I did this until one day she walked by.

"She" was a girl who had recently moved into our neighborhood. I had seen her at school, but thought nothing of her either way. She was very pretty with dark long wavy hair. She was not fancy at all. She liked to wear jeans and flannel shirts. She had pure natural beauty. You could tell she didn't fuss much about her looks, but then again, she didn't need to.

Anyway, she was walking by the bench one day when I was sitting there, likely moping about something and doing homework, and she dropped something out of her pocket. I automatically yelled to her,

"Hey you, you dropped something."

She stopped and looked over at me. She responded, "Hey YOU???" I then said,

"Excuse me madame. I mean ma'am. You appear to have dropped something, Your Highness." She replied,

"That's more like it."

She went back and picked up what she had dropped. Let me just say that to this day I still don't know if she dropped that on purpose or not. But at any rate, she took it upon herself to come over to the bench and have a seat next to me.

In a very over-confident way she said,

"I am new here and looking for new friends; you want to be my new boyfriend?" I replied back to her,

"Sorry I am not interested in girlfriends."

She replied, "I didn't ask you about girlfriends, I asked you to be my boyfriend."

I said, "I think it's the same result."

She said, "That's fine I'm done with boys anyways."

I said, "Good, because I'm done with girls."

At that point there was an awkward but relieving silence.

SILENCE, finally silence.

I had only known her for five minutes and already found her exhausting.

She then said, "Now that we have agreed to hate each other, would it be too awkward for you to show me around this park?"

I just kind of looked at her like I knew what she was doing, but I decided to take the bait anyway because I kind of liked her. She was blunt and honest to the point of being rude. How refreshing! I was so tired of people being nice to my face and then abandoning me like I was trash. Here is someone new treating me like trash right up front so there would be no surprises or disappointments later on.

We both got up from the bench and I led her around the park. I took her to the dark area of the park in the woods to show her the stone post. There was this granite stone post hidden away in a dark corner of the park, and nobody knew what it was, or why it was there. It gave all the kids good reason to come up with all kinds of theories of what might be buried there, or who, or if it was a portal to another universe or something. I thought this new girl had enough of a crazy dark side that maybe she would be intrigued by it. But she seemed more interested in taking jabs at me instead.

We continued to snipe at each other the entire walk. I felt so much at ease. I felt I had known her for years, yet it had only been a very excruciating hour or so. Finally, she said she needed to go home. I went home as well. Then something unexpected happened. I spent half the night lying in bed thinking about her.

I started to ask myself why I was losing sleep over someone who was not even that nice. Why did I find "not nice" attractive? Did I just say "attractive?" I then asked myself why I was using the word "attractive." UGH.

The next day at school I found myself praying I would see her. I did! I found her at her locker and I complimented what a horrible mess her locker was, and I asked her if she kept her life how she kept her locker. She smiled and won the encounter by "checking me out." I saw her eyes go from my eyes down to just below my waist, and then back up to my eyes again. That took away my train of thought and I just used my remaining couple seconds to ask her if she would be at the park after school. Her reply was

"Maybe."

Sure enough, after school she found me sitting on the bench at the park. I was excited and relieved she showed up. We started talking more normally like we didn't hate each other. It was so easy and pleasant. Again, I was so amazed at how at ease I was with her, as if I had always known her. It was NO work at all to talk with her. I didn't have to put on a show, entertain her, or be careful of my words. I could just be me, however stupid, obnoxious, mean, or awkward I might be in the moment. She delivered the same back to me.

I supposed you can see it coming, right? Yeah, I was in love with her. Somehow, we became boyfriend/girlfriend without me wanting it, without me chasing it, without me trying to get it, and without me even asking her. In fact, I never asked her to be my girlfriend. There was no drama like the first time. This time, it was just natural and happened as if I never had a choice. Formalities were not necessary with her. We just "WERE," if that makes any sense. It was perhaps the most unintended relationship in the history of relationships. But it happened.

Like all of my other friends had done, I kind of separated from any casual relationships I had, and focused my entire life on my life with her. It seemed like a perfect balance between focusing on myself and focusing on her. It seemed healthy. Is this what it's like to have a mature adult relationship? We were truly friends who just happened to be a romantic couple as well. I began to think of her as someone I could possibly marry someday.

Another thing that made this relationship very different from my first one was that we did "adult things" together. Yep, she was my "first time." I won't give any details except to tell you it happened at the park one late evening. It was perfect. That's all I will say.

Ironically, I think THIS was the most stable phase of my life to this point. I know I said earlier that I felt more stable alone, but in this case I actually felt more stable in this relationship with her. We were very happy and it went on for quite a while. But there was one major issue I had not considered. She was a year older than me. I was a Junior and she was a Senior. So. Hmmm. Anyone see the problem yet?

The school year was winding down and she was set to graduate high school. I started to get huge anxiety as to what was going to happen after she graduated. I was afraid to discuss it with her, and whenever I dared to bring it up, she just said she was not sure what she was going to do.

The problem is that time was passing, and eventually she would have to know what she was doing. That day came.

One day when we were both sitting at the park, she just came out and said it. She bluntly said, "I'm moving to go to college."

It was like being hit with a board. I asked her "where?".

Of course, it was to another state very far away. I tried to be calm and adult about it, and I said that I knew she would go SOMEWHERE. I then said that she could come back home as often as possible and we could still see each other very often. I added how I only had one more year of high school left, and I could join her at her school, wherever it was.

She didn't reply.

Just silence.

I started to get that familiar dead doom feeling in my stomach.

She then calmly explained that her parents were moving also. She gave me a moment to calculate the meaning of this in my mind. So I said,

"So you are not coming back. You can't come back?"

She didn't answer. Her non-answer was confirmation.

I was shocked. I didn't know what to say. It was weird because we were in love, she wasn't mad at me, and I wasn't mad at her, yet we were going to have to breakup? I was an adult now, and not having a meltdown tantrum from the news, and I could tell she was upset about it also, but trying to be calm as well. Without any words, I think we both decided to just act normal for the remaining time we had together. I will admit there were no more joyous moments after that, but we stayed together. Our remaining time together was solemn, but still filled with love, caring, and respect for each other.

I could tell how soon she would be leaving by her behavior toward me. One Saturday night in the middle of summer, she had that look in her eyes, and asked if we could stay late in the park that night. I knew what that meant. So we did. She brought a blanket and some food. We had a nice afternoon and evening. Then we made love. We made love for the last time. I knew it would be the last time. I knew she designed it this way. I played along. It was sweet and it was intense. But when it was over, I laid on top of her and my eyes started leaking tears. She tried to break the tension by saying,

"If you cry all over my breasts I'll kill you." We both laughed and I pulled it together and laid back next to her. We watched the stars. I told her that no matter what happens in life, we will always be looking at the same stars together.

We laid there for a while and then she said we could see each other in the morning before she left if I wanted. I was silent and didn't know what to answer. I knew if I saw her the morning she was leaving, I would fall apart and it would be very painful and dramatic. So I said to her,

"I want my memory of our time together to be this perfect moment."

She seemed a bit disappointed that I might not want to see her in the morning. But she didn't understand that I would completely fall apart and just cry and melt if I did. I knew this was the best way. Well, there is no best way, is there? There is just a way. A not good way. Endings are not good no matter how they end.

Believe it or not, our evening ended peacefully and calmly. We kissed each other gently and took turns saying "I love you." Then I turned away to leave. She then came over to me and kissed me gently one last time. She whispered in my ear,

"You are the best non-boyfriend I ever had and ever will have."

I was going to cry. I was trying to say the same thing mutually back to her, but I was going to cry.

She put her finger over her mouth to tell me not to speak.

And she walked away.

And I walked away.

The next morning I had this overwhelming urge to see her one last time. I quickly got dressed and started running over to her house. But when I got there, she was gone. They must have left early after I decided not to meet with her that morning. Everything was gone. They had moved. She was gone.

I went to the park. I sat on the bench. And I cried. But I did not cry like a baby. I did not cry out of hurt or being damaged. I cried out of gratitude. What a wonderful incredible amazing relationship that was. I was so lucky. Yet I cried. Once again, I was alone.

I mourned that relationship for a long time. However, I was more adult about it. I knew not to TRY and find another girlfriend, and I knew not to try and NOT find another girlfriend. I knew to just "be," and life would dish out whatever it decided. I clung to the one thing in my life that gave me comfort and peace: the park. I realized that the park was the one thing in my life that never disappointed me or abandoned me. Despite my intense loneliness, I kept going to the park to sit on the bench and do my homework and my thinking.

Fortunately for me, there were big changes coming for me also. I was going into my last year of high school and I had big choices to make. Thankfully, that would occupy my mind most of the time, and although I never got over my second relationship, I was able to function as a normal young adult trying to grow up and find his way into the world.

However, there would be another event to rock my world before that phase of my life was over. Although I never got along with my parents very well, I absolutely adored my grandmother. My mother couldn't stand her, and my grandmother seemed to take joy in torturing my mother. The two got along about as well as I got along with MY parents. But to me, she was always kind, accommodating, and ready to spoil me.

But she was old and in very poor health. I knew her time would be coming to an end soon. Finally, as if right on cue to land another blow on my chin, my mother came to my room and told me the news. Grandma had passed away. She just stared at me waiting for a reaction. I had none. So she walked out. I know my mother was likely dealing with her own issues and feelings regarding the death, and so was I. My reaction was to just walk out of the house and go to the park.

I sat on the bench and started talking to Grandma. Don't worry, I didn't talk out loud (although there is nothing wrong with that by the way). I talked to her in my head. Similar to how I handled the recent news of my girlfriend moving away, and also a prior loss of a dear neighbor, and other hard losses I had, I chose to respond with gratitude rather than total sadness, anger, or whatever else people do. I thanked her for being a great Grandma. I thanked her for being the one family member who never judged me, and just loved me instead.

Then I started to think to myself.

Had I just lost the last person on Earth who did not judge me or constantly criticize me for things?

Was I totally alone with just the savage beasts now?

I think I had an epiphany that night in the park on the bench. I think I realized that I was no longer a child. I was an adult. I say this because I realized that I was likely alone, in the respect that I would be the only one to love me for who I was, rather than what others thought I should be.

I learned the concept of self-love.

Perhaps that was the final gift my grandmother left for me.

I spent my last year in high school, and at home, as an adult due to this, and other major incidences in my life. Meaning, I was an adult inside myself for that final year. I think even my parents saw this, and they gave up on hounding me. The game was over. Give it up.

Thank goodness they did. My final year was fairly peaceful toward the end, and I was very focused on school and all of the events last-year students partake in. I was social while still being very reserved within myself. I was no longer seeking anything from anyone, but at the same time was willing to show interest and kindness toward others who would show the same toward me.

I had decided that the best thing for me might be to attend a university as far from home as possible. I needed to experience some independence from the life that had been molded around me in my hometown. Thus, I knew my days at home in my hometown were numbered. I knew my days at the park were numbered. To be honest, my biggest anxiety about moving far way, was leaving the park behind, in addition to a couple key people in my life.

Because of that, I spent a lot of time sitting at the park that last year. I spent a lot of time noticing the details of the park, the grass, the trees, and even the bench. I wanted to be able to remember every detail of it all. I noticed how the grass was EXACTLY the same as it was when I was a little child. I noticed how the trees were noticeably bigger, but that I had only noticed it for the first time in this moment. Then I noticed the bench.

The bench was shiny and brand new when I was a small child. That sweet old lady, Mrs. Carlisle, who donated the bench after her husband died, had given me so much by donating that bench, in addition to giving me my soul back during the year at The Lake.

But the bench had aged in all the years I was growing up. It was no longer shiny. Kids had carved names and stuff in the wood, and the wood was a darker color than the very light color it was when it was new. Everything had aged. I had aged. Things were the same, but everything was different. It was time for me to move on with my life. Nothing lasts forever, and everything eventually changes.

I indeed moved away, only thanks to the generosity of some very special people who had changed my life. I moved to the opposite side of the country. I went to a university, did lots of traveling, and built my own independent life during the years I was able to live there.

Time seemed to escalate faster and faster with each passing year. I was 18 when I left home, then I was 21, then 25, then 30, then 35. My goodness, make it stop. It never stopped.

During those years, I came back home very often, and sometimes for long periods of time. My reasons varied, from personal to business. Whenever I returned home, I would always go sit at the park. It was so funny because the grass, the trees, everything, always seemed to get a little smaller each year. It's like the park was shrinking. The bench remained the same size, but kept getting older. I would always sit and contemplate at how my childhood was, and what my adulthood turned out to be. Most of the people I had known as a child were gone. So once again, I felt I was the only one there. I was alone. But there was something about visiting the park and sitting there that made me feel I was never alone. I was grateful for this.

The years continued to race by. I lived my life, doing as much good as I possibly could do, with the blessings that had been bestowed upon me. Eventually, I lost my parents, in addition to others. I grieved with gratitude rather than sadness. I think sadness had been in me for my entire life, but I chose to not allow it to be the dominant emotion. I chose gratitude, even while deep inside I might have felt sadness.

I think I learned after my first breakup, that sadness was not the answer. Sadness only results in sadness. But gratitude allows for hope that more blessings or good things can come in the future. There is no escaping sadness, but if a person leads with gratitude, they can look for the future blessings to come. There are always blessings if you look for them. There is always sadness, even if you don't look for it. So why bother looking for sadness if it's always going to find you anyway? It is smarter to look for the blessings since they can be harder to spot. Does that make sense?

As I became much older, I eventually moved back to my hometown on a permanent basis. Perhaps I was just the proverbial salmon swimming back up stream from whence it came. I think I wanted the familiar peace of the park. The park was a place I had known since a very small child, where I felt continuity in my life, and a place that never let me down or hurt me. I found myself hobbling over to the park to sit on the bench almost daily. I would just sit, watch all the kids play, and think. I seriously could not believe that I was watching these little kids play in the park, and it seemed just like yesterday that I was one of the little kids playing there. What happened? Where did the years go? How did I get this old?

Speaking of old, I started to notice the old bench was falling apart. One of the wood strips on the back was totally broken off. The wood straps on the seat portion looked like they could give way at any moment. It looked like people had tried to paint the bench over and over through the years, thinking the paint would hold the rotting wood together. But I had an idea!

I went to the town office and spoke to the person in charge of the parks. I decided not to tell them who I was, or what I had been involved in. I just briefly told them I had grown up there and had recently moved back permanently. I explained that the park was important to me. The person was perhaps half my age, had no idea who I was, and was likely wondering why I was bothering to explain all of these things that they had no interest in hearing. I got to the point and asked if it would be possible for me to donate a new bench for the park.

The person seemed surprised by my offer, and said nobody had ever done that before. I corrected the young man and said that many years ago, way before he was born, a very nice older lady, whose name he should certainly know well, had indeed donated a bench before, and that the bench she donated was the one currently sitting there. I told him the condition of the bench was such that it would have to be demolished and taken away before too long, and that I didn't want there to be no bench there. I told him there MUST be a bench in that

EXACT location.

I am fairly certain by now that the man was starting to think I was senile, and these were just the ramblings of a crazy old man. So, I tried to calm down and keep to simple facts. I once again asked if I could donate a new bench to REPLACE the bench that was there. It was not an additional bench. It was a replacement. He understood and agreed the current bench likely needed replacement.

We made the arrangements, and I donated the funds without hesitation. Once they figured out who I was, others in the office spoke up and said there would be a plaque placed on the bench with my name on it. I hesitated, but then said that would be fine. I wasn't even sure I wanted a plaque with my name on it, because the bench I had known, never had a plaque with a name on it, except for when the bench was brand new. The plaque had been removed shortly after it was installed. I wanted an EXACT replacement, but I said I was okay with the plaque. I knew by this point, they all thought I had turned into a grumpy crazy old man, but when you get to be the age of a grumpy crazy old man, you don't care what people think, and you just start to play the role, even though inside you are not a grumpy crazy old man. Oh, there I go rambling again. Never mind.

I made sure to ask when the old bench would be taken away. I did not verbalize it to them, but I felt I needed to say goodbye to it, and I didn't want to miss that chance. The day came when I had to make sure I went to the park to say goodbye to the old bench. I quietly sat on the bench looking out at the park. Similar to what I had done after the passing of so many very dear people to me, I thanked the bench for all it had given me. I started to think of all the moments the bench had played in my life. I remembered being nine years old and sitting there eating ice cream with my friends. I remembered my first girlfriend. I remembered I had my first kiss on that bench. I remembered I met my second girlfriend at that bench. I remembered all of the people who played such a pivotal role in my life. I especially remembered my 'Grandpa' who allowed me options in life, in addition to my most important mentor at the farm in the countryside, who had shaped who I was, and what I was to become. I remembered the Carlisles, whose bench was the focal point of my entire childhood, including nearly all the memories I cherished. Of course, I remembered and gave thanks for the Carlisles shaping my life in such an incredible way that they would never fully realize. I remembered everything, both the good and the bad.

Then I had a panic. I had this sudden thought that I could not have this old bench removed. This old bench was my entire life. My entire life, or at least my entire childhood, played out on this bench. Removing this bench meant my whole life would be gone. I began thinking that this bench was all I had left of my childhood. Even my parents were gone. Everything from my earliest years were gone. But the bench was still here. I had to keep it. I literally panicked.

However, good sense finally got a hold of me. I realized that this was not a matter of choice. The bench was too old to be used. It had to go. I also realized that my childhood and my life were not within the bench. My life was within my memories. My life was within me. My life was within all of the good I had been able to give others. I was the one to allow things to live on. It was not the responsibility of the bench. It was MY responsibility to let the past live on into the future. It was that moment when I realized replacing the old bench with a new bench would indeed provide a way for the past to live on into the future. It would allow a whole new generation to enjoy the same things that I enjoyed. I knew it was the right thing to do. Just as I did with my second girlfriend, I stood up, blew a kiss toward the bench, and I walked away.

I didn't want to see the old bench being destroyed, so I purposely stayed away from the park for about a week while the replacement was being installed. After I was assured the new bench was in place, I went to the park to see the new bench. I was delighted!

The new bench was EXACTLY like the old bench, sitting in the EXACT same location, except the new bench was brand new and shiny. It literally looked EXACTLY how it looked the first time I noticed it when I was a small child. But there was more. I noticed where they had installed the plaque on the bench that was supposed to have my name on it. But guess what? Some kid had already pried off the plaque, and the plaque was gone. HA! I started laughing. My first thought was, "PERFECT." Then I laughed some more.

But that was not it. I noticed out of the corner of my eye some kind of board laying in the bushes in back of the bench area. I hobbled over to investigate. I immediately recognized it as one of the strapping boards from the old bench. I picked it up and caressed it as if it was a dirty lost puppy or something. I took it home with me. To this day, I have that board from the old bench sitting in my living room where I can look at it and touch it anytime I want.

As for the new bench, I started back up with my daily walks to the park, and spent plenty of time sitting on the bench watching life go by. Or actually, I prefer to say "watching life happen." Sometimes I notice the kids in the park looking at me and saying something to each other. I know they are likely talking about me the same way me and my friends used to talk about that amazing sweet old lady on the bench so many years ago. I don't mind. I just sit on the bench and watch them play.

More recently, I was at the park sitting there and I noticed a nice teenage couple walking by. I had been watching them for a while. I could tell they were in love, and enjoying their time together. When they got near to the bench, they noticed I was still sitting there. I quickly realized that they had planned on sitting on the bench together, but me still being there was ruining their plans. They started to walk by me. I quickly called out to them, "WAIT!" They turned around and wondered why I was yelling at them. I said to them, "I was just leaving. Please, sit on the bench, it's okay." They responded by saying, "Sir, this is your bench, we don't want to disturb you." I replied to them, "No. This is YOUR bench. It's my time to leave. Please come sit and live your life."

I'm sure they thought I was crazy, but I didn't care. I managed to get up without my knees giving out, and I started to walk away. They sat down and immediately started sitting close and talking as if they were the only two people on Earth. I knew I had done the right thing.

I had done the right thing by getting up and leaving. But I had also done the right thing by donating the new bench for the next generation to enjoy. The new bench allowed for my life, and all of the lives of everyone who used it before me, to be remembered, and to live on. I had made it possible for another generation, or more, to enjoy the same bench in the same location as I did, and those who came before me did. By giving others the chance to live the experiences I lived, I am in a way keeping all of my experiences and memories alive. It's not just the bench that will still be sitting there long after I am gone. It is the life experiences of the young people that will continue on, long after I am gone. In this way, my youth, and all of my most precious moments, will live on forever by virtue of the next generations living the same precious moments as I did there on the bench. Life is not about what you had. Life is about what you enable to continue onward through others, long after you are gone.

If you ever see a bench at a park, please have a seat and think about how you can live your life to the fullest, while paying it forward and helping the next generation continue the legacy of precious youth.

And by the way. I was never alone. I always had myself, my dreams, my experiences, my memories, and my love for enabling all of that to continue beyond me.

As long as you continue to pay it forward and give of yourself to others, you never get old inside, and you never die. You continue on through them into the future.

You live on, just like the bench.

CHAPTER TWO

The Grumpy Old Man

From very early on as a child, I was aware of the old man who lived down the street. Some of the kids called him "Old Man Wilkens," while others called him "The Mean Old Man," but the polite name was "Mr. Wilkens." The adults seemed to just leave him alone and not speak of him much, but he had a horrible reputation among the kids in the neighborhood.

He was *THAT* grumpy old man who would literally yell "GET OFF MY LAWN," if for some reason kids parked their bikes on the edge of his lawn and talked. For some games, like frisbee, we would use multiple lawns in the neighborhood to have enough space, and if we spent too much time on Mr. Wilkens's lawn, he would first poke his head through the curtains and scowl, and then about fourteen seconds later, he would open his front door, and stand looking as scary as possible. That usually worked in getting all the kids to scatter off his lawn. If it didn't, that is when he would do the "GET OFF MY LAWN" thing.

None of the kids liked him, and he didn't seem to have any friends amongst the adults either. He lived alone and never had visitors. He never left his house except for the rare times he would be seen sitting on the bench at the park very early in the morning, or every Friday morning to do his grocery shopping. I know this because his car would be gone at the exact time every Friday, and then he would return and have to make exactly three trips from his car to his front door in order to get all the grocery bags in.

The only other time you would ever see him outside was when he mowed his lawn, and he would usually do that early in the morning before anyone was around to see him doing it. He never socialized and he had no pets. Truly, the old man was kind of a mystery actually. He seemed to have always lived there, but none of the older people in the neighborhood ever spoke of him.

Really, all we knew for sure is that he hated kids and was mean. That's all we knew. Some of the kids seemed to enjoy intentionally annoying him. I used to see some of the kids whisper and snicker to each other just before pulling up with their bicycles onto his lawn. I think they used to place bets on how long it would take before Mr. Wilkens would come out yelling at them. Then the kids would scatter while they were laughing. Although I had no reason to believe the old man was nothing but mean, I also thought it was equally mean how some of the kids treated him.

I think what struck me even more was how the entire neighborhood of adults would completely ignore him. During the Christmas holiday, most neighbors exchanged dishes of treats and cookies and things. You could see almost every neighbor would have some kind of treats left outside their door, but never Mr. Wilkens's. Nobody ever left anything for Mr. Wilkens. Even the mail delivery person avoided direct contact with him. Whenever anyone else in the neighborhood had a package, the mail person would knock on the door, and there might be a thirty second exchange of pleasant conversation. But with Mr. Wilkens, the mail person would just knock on his door and leave the package outside his door, and quickly scurry away before Mr. Wilkens could answer the door.

I could understand why the kids didn't like him, but I was always intrigued as to why all of the so-called civilized adults also did not like him. Nobody ever told us kids that he was dangerous or a criminal or anything. It didn't appear that Mr. Wilkens had done anything wrong to anyone. How could he? He never went anywhere or had any contact with anyone. He was kind of harmless when you think about it.

To be honest, I became kind of intrigued with him. How could one man be so mysterious, hate kids so much, and also have adults dislike him, all while he seemingly did nothing wrong to anyone, ever. Perhaps I was just a curious naïve child, but I was always interested in the psychology of how people treated each other. Like, why did some kids get picked on, while other kids were seen as heroes? Human psychology was fascinating to me, even at a very young age.

Even so, I avoided Mr. Wilkens.

I never caused him any aggravation or taunted him like the other kids. But I also made sure to never get near his property or step on his lawn. I wasn't necessarily afraid of him, but I also didn't want to get yelled at either. However, one day I ended up violating my own rules of avoidance.

A few of us were kicking a ball around in the street, when one of the kids kicked the ball too hard, and it went flying past me and well onto Mr. Wilkens's lawn. All of us looked at each other at the same time, almost as if to say "what now?" Since I was closest to the ball, and was the one it flew past, it was obvious to everyone, and to me, that it would be me who needed to go and get the ball. I took a deep breath and gently walked onto his lawn and over to the ball in order to retrieve it. It was as if Mr. Wilkens had been peeking out of his window for hours waiting for this exact situation to happen, he flung open his door and yelled,

"HEY!"

I froze and was kind of waiting for the "GET OFF MY LAWN" part, but instead he just said,

"DON'T PLAY ON MY LAWN, IT HURTS MY GRASS."

Instead of just grabbing the ball and running away like all the other kids always did, I yelled back at him,

"I'm sorry, we will try."

Mr. Wilkens seemed kind of surprised by my civil response. He just grunted and shut his door. The other kids just laughed at me since I had to deal with Mr. Wilkens.

I managed to avoid any further run-ins with Mr. Wilkens for quite a long time until one fateful day when I happened to witness a mishap with his mail. Specifically, it was a package delivery. It was a really windy day, and as usual the mail delivery person just left a package for Mr. Wilkens outside his door. It must have been a very light package, because the wind blew it off his steps, then into his driveway, then out into the street. Me and a few friends were walking down the street and noticed the package sitting out in the street.

It was another kid who picked it up and read the label to see whose it was. He said in a slow voice, "Willllkens." I said, "Oh, Mr. Wilkens!" My friends asked what we should do with it. Everyone was looking at each other as if this was one of the world's most difficult puzzles to solve. I said, "We should give it to him." They all at the same time were saying "no way," "forget it," "you're crazy," and stuff like that. Then one of my friends said, "YOU give it to him." They all looked at me like this was some kind of a thrown-down dare challenge, like a duel to the death or something, and I had to decide if I was man enough to accept the challenge. I kind of thought they were being silly. I had always thought all along everyone was being over-dramatic about Mr. Wilkens to be honest. So I just said, "Okay fine, I'll give it to him."

I grabbed the package and started walking over to Mr. Wilkens's house. My friends yelled out across the street that I couldn't just leave it outside his door. I had to actually give it to him directly. That was part of the challenge. I just kept walking like I was ignoring their nonsense. I was going to do that anyway.

I walked all the way up to Mr. Wilkens's door and was kind of surprised he had not come out yelling at me yet. I paused, and knocked. About ten seconds later Mr. Wilkens opened the door. He saw me standing there, and he just stared at me. I think he was in shock that a kid would be standing there outside his door, and I think I was in shock that he was not yelling at me by now.

He finally said, "Yes?"

I lifted up the package I was holding a little higher and explained to him that his package must have blown away, and that I had found it out in the street. He just stared at me again like he was in even more shock. I held the package out toward him, and he reached out and took it from me. I expected him to then promptly slam the door in my face, so I took a cautionary step backwards so that the door wouldn't break my nose when he slammed it in my face.

Instead, he kept the door open and examined the package to verify it was his, and to see where it was from on the return label. He looked at the return address and seemed to recognize it as something he had been expecting. He looked back at me and said,

"This was very kind of you to bring this to me boy."

I was so surprised by his words that I didn't know what to say.
I just said, "No problem, Sir."
He looked at me more closely, grunted, and then said,
"Well thank you," and with that he closed the door, and did so in a normal gentle way.

I turned around and walked back to my friends, who were anxiously waiting to hear my report of exactly what happened, including every word that was exchanged. They seemed to be surprised that I had escaped certain death. All I said to them was, "It really was no big deal." With that, they seemed too embarrassed to continue the game, as it had backfired on them, and it proved to be a bunch of nothing.

My next run-in with Mr. Wilkens would happen by chance on a Friday morning. Mr. Wilkens had just returned home from his weekly grocery shopping trip, and I happened to be walking down the street to meet with some friends.

As I was walking by Mr. Wilkens's driveway, I saw one of his grocery bags rip out through the bottom, and all his groceries spilled out onto the driveway next to his car. Without hesitation I ran over to him and said, "I can help pick this up if you want." He looked at me, and I could tell he immediately recognized me as the kid who had brought him his mail package from before. So, I got a quite friendly,

"Sure boy, thanks!"

I gathered up his groceries, including cans that had rolled under his car. By the time I was done, he had come out with a new bag to put them in. I put everything in the new bag and started carrying the bag of groceries to his front door. I did not really think through what I was doing, because at this rate I was going to be bringing the bag inside his house.

Surely, I should not go into his house.
I might never be heard from again.
That's like walking into the belly of the beast.
Nobody makes it out alive.

But I realized my thoughts were those of my friends talking, and not real life, so I calmed my inner thoughts. Sure enough, Mr. Wilkens held the door open so that I could bring the groceries inside the house. I naturally followed him to the kitchen.

To my knowledge, NOBODY had EVER been inside Mr. Wilkens's house. Me being inside his house was the equivalent of being the only human to see Big Foot or some other legendary creature up close. This was like the Holy Grail of legendary lore among the kids in the neighborhood. Yet, here I was, and none of the other kids were around to witness it. They would never believe it happened. Regardless, I made a point of taking a very good, long, and close look at everything around me.

I was very surprised by what I saw. I had expected a dark, gloomy, old, and dirty monster's lair, with hints of ancient victims, body parts, and skeletons, hidden in the closets or under the coffee table. Instead, I was seeing a very nice home.

In fact, his home was much nicer than mine. All of the furniture was super nice and kept in perfect condition. His house was spotless inside. He had lots of nice things, antique vases, and TONS of pictures all over his walls. There were way too many pictures for me to focus on and take them all in at once, but they appeared to be pictures of a man (him?) in all different kinds of locations around the world. I tried to look more, but Mr. Wilkens was already trying to lead me back to the front door and out of his house. We reached the door and he said, "Thank you for your kindness, boy." I said it was no problem, and I walked out. He then proceeded to take inside the rest of the groceries by himself.

It was only several days later when I was walking by Mr. Wilkens's house, and he must have been watching out for me, because he managed to get to the door and open it before I had passed his house. He yelled to me,

"HEY BOY!"

I waved at him and walked over to his door. He told me that he had a reward for me in return for helping with the groceries the other day. He asked me if I liked ice cream sandwiches, and I said "yes!"

He told me to wait and he would bring one out to me. I waited on his steps, and thirty seconds later he came out with an ice cream sandwich. He motioned for me to sit on the steps and he said,

"You can eat it here."

I sat down and started in on the ice cream treat. He seemed to watch me to make sure I was enjoying it. I was almost through the entire ice cream when he asked me if I knew how to play checkers. I was surprised by the question but responded that I had played it before. Without a word he went back inside his house and came back out with a checkers set. He started setting it up at a little table he kept outside by his door.

When I finished my ice cream I went over to his table and sat down. He went first. We played checkers and it was not long before he had beaten me. He was pretty smart and clever for an old man. He said,

"Let's try again!" But this time, he started to critique every move I made. He told me why the move would not work out well, and guided me to make other moves. This time, I beat him, but it was obvious he let me win, in addition to the obvious fact he told me all the moves to make anyways. He said,

"Try again!" But when he was resetting the board, it started to rain all of a sudden. It wasn't just raining, it was POURING. We both ran into his house. He got me a little towel so I could dry off the little bit I had gotten wet.

He then said, "You better tell your mother where you are so she doesn't worry. You can use my phone." I responded,

"It's okay, my mom will know that I went inside a friend's house because of the rain, and I don't have to be home until later."

Mr. Wilkens responded, "Yes, but you are not at a friend's house, and I don't want her to worry."

I paused and said, "Yes, I AM at a friend's house."

Mr. Wilkens paused as if he had to fully process what I had just said. He grunted and just said,

"Okay."

He looked at me, and I think was wondering what in the world he was going to do with some kid in his house with no way to get rid of him, because of the rain. I solved his problem by seizing this golden opportunity to start looking at all the pictures he had on his living room wall. I could tell he was a little nervous with me looking at all of them, but he said nothing.

I started asking him questions about them. I asked if the man in the pictures was him, and he said, "Yes!" I asked where all these places where in the pictures. He told me they were from all over the world from all of his travels. I was so fascinated that I got lost in it all. I kept looking at everything until Mr. Wilkens pointed out that the rain had stopped. He said again that he didn't want my mother to worry. I said okay, and slowly made it to the door. On my way out he said,

"When you come back again, we will move on to chess."

I smiled and took that as an invitation and said, "Yes for sure."

Very quickly, word had gotten around that I had been inside the belly of the beast and had survived the encounter. Kids were asking me how I managed to make it inside, and asked how I managed to live through it all. I just laughed them all off. *Silly little children*. Then someone had said how they had seen me playing checkers with the mean old man. I responded by saying he is not mean, and he is way smarter than any of them.

I think my friends thought I was weird for interacting with Mr. Wilkens, but I really didn't care. I really liked it. I didn't have a Grandpa, and being with Mr. Wilkens was kind of like having a Grandpa. I was not going to let comments from my friends take that away from me.

It wasn't long before I decided to cash-in on my invitation from Mr. Wilkens to come back. So, I walked over to his house and knocked on his door. He answered and smiled, but seemed to not know why I was there. I broke the awkward moment by saying,

"Hey you said I could come over to play chess."

Mr. Wilkens seemed highly amused by this as if he never expected me to actually accept his invitation. He said,

"Then come in boy." He asked if I wanted a drink, and he got out his chess set.

I didn't know much about chess, and he could immediately see this for himself. He proceeded to coach me through each move like he did with checkers. After a long session of chess, I told him I was too tired to play again and I stood up. I started walking around the living room and looking at everything again. The truth is that I was far more interested in all his stuff and pictures than I was in learning how to play chess.

I spotted several pictures that looked super old, but were of some cool looking teenager. I was wondering who that was, so I asked Mr. Wilkens. I said,

"Who is this really cool looking kid?"

Mr. Wilkens laughed and said, "That's Henry."

I asked who Henry was, and he replied, "I'm Henry."

I said, "THAT'S YOU???"

Mr. Wilkens just nodded in the affirmative. I was stunned. I had seriously only thought of Mr. Wilkens as an ancient old man. Surely he was never young at any point. AND Mr. Wilkens ALSO had a FIRST name?? I really couldn't wrap my head around all this.

I looked at the pictures more closely. In the pictures he looked like one of those teenagers who was super popular at school and always got the girls he wanted. I looked at the pictures, and then looked back at Mr. Wilkens, and then looked back at the pictures again. I did this several times. I think Mr. Wilkens was starting to get embarrassed and said, "That was a very long time ago." I didn't want to annoy him, so I stopped and moved onto other things.

I looked at his closet and the door was open. I could kind of see what looked like some kind of military uniform jacket, maybe from the Army or something. I went over to the closet to take a closer look. I tried to peer all the way into the closet without touching anything. To open the door more, or move any of the garments inside, would be overly nosey and rude, but seeing everything you can see without touching, is fair game.

Mr. Wilkens saw this and asked me what I was looking at. I asked him about the military jacket in the closet. He paused, slowly made his way over to the closet, and pulled out the jacket. Once it was fully out of the closet and I was able to see it more clearly, I could see it was covered with medals. I said to him,

"WOW, are those all YOUR medals?"

He just said "Yep!"

I asked how he got them, and he said he got some of them during the war, but a lot of them after the war.

He then added, "Most of the guys who deserved all the medals were killed before they could be given them."

He didn't at all seem proud of them. It was almost as if he was embarrassed by them. After he felt I had a good look at the jacket, he put it back into the closet and seemed relieved to do so.

I started spending more and more time with Mr. Wilkens. I split my time between my friends, school, and Mr. Wilkens. My parents were fully aware of my friendship with him and seemed okay with it, although confused as to why it would be appealing to me. I didn't talk to my parents much about it until Christmas season rolled around.

As usual, my mother was making all kinds of Christmas treats, and was preparing a huge amount of Christmas trays that she would disperse to all the neighbors. When they were nearly complete, I asked her which tray was for Mr. Wilkens. She paused and said,

"We don't really know Mr. Wilkens and have never given him a tray in the past." She added, "Plus, Mr. Wilkens has never participated in the exchange of Christmas trays within the neighborhood."

My mom could see I was immediately disturbed by her answer and explanations. I said to her,

"I know Mr. Wilkens, and Mr. Wilkens needs a Christmas tray; I will give it to him myself." My mother hesitated as if wondering whether to oppose me on this or just go along with it. Fortunately, she decided to make it easier on both of us by going along with it. She started digging around and gathering stray scraps and leftovers of treats she had not put into trays already. She started just throwing anything she could find onto his tray. I stopped her and told her that Mr. Wilkens wouldn't eat those, but would eat these other ones, and so on and so forth.

My mom for maybe the fifth time hesitated and just looked at me like she was really annoyed. She then said,

"Why does Mr. Wilkens mean so much to you?"

My answer to her was, "I never had a Grandpa, and Mr. Wilkens is like my Grandpa. Plus Mr. Wilkens is the most interesting person I have ever met in my life."

My mom paused AGAIN, and gave me *THAT LOOK* again, and said, "Well that's quite a statement."

I just said "Yeah." At last, she seemed to give up the fight, and I helped her assemble a really nice Christmas plate that I knew Mr. Wilkens would enjoy.

When it was time for all the neighbors to exchange the Christmas trays, my mom had taken ALL of the trays that she was going to deliver door to door, but left the one for Mr. Wilkens on the kitchen counter for me to get. I took it and walked over to Mr. Wilkens's house. I could see multiple Christmas platters at many of the neighbor's houses. I got to Mr. Wilkens's house and of course no Christmas trays were at his door as usual. I knocked on his door and he answered. He immediately saw the Christmas tray in my hand. He smiled and told me to come in.

He said "What's this?"

I said, "It's your Christmas tray."

He replied, "Nobody ever gives me a Christmas tray, and I don't give out trays."

I said, "Well you get a Christmas tray now."

He took the tray from me, turned his back to me in order to set it down, and he paused. I thought I saw his hand reach up to maybe wipe his eye. He kept his back to me for another thirty seconds pretending to fiddle with something.

He then turned around and said, "Thank you boy!"

He added, "I assume this was put together by your mother, so could you please thank her for me also."

I said "Sure." Then I said, "Merry Christmas."

Time went by and my fascination with Mr. Wilkens never faded. I continued to visit him, and I think he came to expect and even depend on my visits as well. I think he had been lonely before, but maybe didn't realize how lonely he was until he was no longer lonely because of my visits. I feel he had been used to his life and was fine with it. But now I was hoping that I was making his life less lonely, and a little better. He was certainly doing that for my life.

Our visits would often start with him trying to start a checkers or chess game, but honestly I was way more interested in his life, and I made every excuse possible to set aside the checkers and chess games in favor of looking through his pictures and asking him questions.

One day I asked him why he had traveled so much. He told me that after the war, he had a different job with the military that had him traveling all over the world. I asked him what his job was and he just stared at me.

Okay, I guess it was a secret?

However, one interesting thing he did say was that everyone should travel as much as possible so that they can appreciate how much better staying at home is. I didn't really understand that until I was much older as an adult. With that said, it did seem that his world travels were important to him, and he was never shy about enthusiastically discussing them, unlike his secrecy regarding his military career. It was all just so endlessly fascinating to me. I had never traveled anywhere beyond the next city over to buy school clothes at the mall each year.

One day Mr. Wilkens turned the tables and started asking ME questions. He never did this. His question was

"What do your friends think about you spending so much time with me?"

I paused and decided to tell the truth. I answered, "They don't understand it at all, and sometimes they make fun of me."

He asked why. I explained that my friends were "not sure about him" (my polite way of telling him that my friends couldn't stand him). I told him how my friends prefer playing amongst themselves and don't understand why I would rather be with an adult (I left out "old man").

Mr. Wilkens asked, "Why do you continue to visit me if you are getting picked on for doing it?"

I replied, "I don't care what they say to me. They are just children. You and I have a sophisticated grown-up relationship."

Mr. Wilkens erupted in laughter. I don't think I had seen him laugh before. Usually I only got a grunt or a smile at best. He then said,

That is a very sophisticated and mature answer."

As another school year was coming to a close before the summer vacation, I ended up spending a lot more time on my school work. Many weeks went by without me seeing Mr. Wilkens. However, as soon as my end-of-year exams were done, I went over to see Mr. Wilkens. I knocked on the door, and there was no answer. I knew he was home because his car was there and it wasn't Friday morning. I stayed and kept knocking more. He finally answered the door. I was a bit stunned by what I saw. He seemed so much older all of a sudden. He looked a bit frail and like ten years older, even though it had only been a couple months since I had seen him last. He had some kind of bandages on his arms where they usually stick those needles in for medicine bags (IV bags) that hang on those poles for sick people. He waved me inside and I walked inside.

His house seemed more messy than usual. Normally Mr. Wilkens kept an immaculate house with everything clean and orderly. I could tell he had not cleaned in a while. He invited me to sit down on the couch. I looked at him and asked how he was doing. It was an awkward question because I could clearly see he was doing horrible, but I didn't know what else to say. However, he actually replied that he was doing fine and he was glad to see me. I told him I had been busy with school, and we talked about my exams and school ending. Then there was a pause.

I finally got the courage and I asked, "Are you sick or something?" He answered, "Well, I don't want to concern you or scare you with unpleasant things." I said to him, "I want to know how you are doing because we are friends." He smiled his usual smile, hesitated a moment, and he said,

"I have a disease."

I asked, "What disease?"

He said, "I have cancer."

I was silent and didn't know what to say next. I just looked down at the floor. Then I asked,

"So how long will it take before you are okay again?"

It was then his turn to not know what to say, and he looked down at the floor. He finally looked at me and said, "I don't know."

When I went back home, I went straight to my mother and told her Mr. Wilkens had cancer. She looked at me as if she already knew this. She said, "Are you okay?" I processed that interaction and realized she had known somehow, and was waiting for this moment when I would find out. I told her I was fine but that I would be spending more time with Mr. Wilkens to help him through his illness. My mom just smiled, as if for the first time since I met Mr. Wilkens, she was finally approving, and even proud of me.

I went over to Mr. Wilkens's house almost every day. He didn't seem to be getting better. He would stay the same for a while, but then get much worse, then stay the same for a while. He never got better though. Instead of playing checkers or chess, I started cleaning his house for him. I knew exactly how he liked to keep things, so it was the perfect arrangement because I knew how he wanted everything kept, and I did the best job I could. But afterwards, I would sit on the couch and ask him my normal annoying questions about his life.

One day I learned something about Mr. Wilkens that I could not have even imagined. I had randomly picked up one of his photo albums that was buried under a bunch of others. I started looking at all the photos. They were mostly photos of some kid. The kid actually looked similar to Mr. Wilkens in those other pictures on the wall. I assumed maybe these were photos of Mr. Wilkens when he was a bit younger than in the other photos. In these photos he looked to be about my age. I asked Mr. Wilkens if these were pictures of him younger.

Mr. Wilkens peeked over to see which album and pictures I was looking at. When he saw, he grew very still and solemn. It was weird.

He said, "No."

I said, "This is NOT you?"

He paused and kind of stumbled and said, "That was my son."

I was stunned and didn't know what to say. I kept looking at the pictures. I asked,

"What's his name?"

He replied, "His name was Peter."

I asked, "Where is Peter now?"

Mr. Wilkens knew this question was coming, and calmly said, "We lost Peter a very long time ago." I asked how. He said, "In a car accident."

I felt I shouldn't ask more.

But this opened up more questions. I couldn't help myself, and I asked, "What happened to Peter's mother?" Mr. Wilkens sighed and appeared to be getting exhausted by the difficult questions. He answered, "Peter's mother couldn't handle his death and had major problems, and eventually also passed away." Once again, I felt I better not ask more questions.

I just kept looking at the pictures of Peter and said WITHOUT THINKING,

"I bet you were a great father."

Mr. Wilkens took in my statement, but then turned away from me and appeared to be cleaning his glasses. With no response, I moved on and kept looking at the pictures. Mr. Wilkens eventually turned back over to me and said,

"You remind me of Peter, he was a lot like you."

I smiled and took that as perhaps the highest compliment anyone had ever given me. I had no words and just kept looking at the pictures.

It turned out that doing Mr. Wilkens's house cleaning wasn't the only thing I would end up doing. I quickly noticed that his grass was getting very long. He obviously was not mowing it anymore, and I kind of felt foolish for not anticipating this and offering to help him. So, I asked him where he kept his lawn mower and that I needed to mow his lawn. I didn't offer or ask. I just TOLD him I needed to mow his grass. I knew how to handle Mr. Wilkens by now. I knew if I offered or asked, he would make some excuse to not accept my offer. Thus, having phrased the question properly, he had no choice but to simply show me where he kept everything and he just said,

"Thank you boy!"

I started mowing his lawn every week. I knew how important his lawn was to him, so I wanted to keep it as nice as he was used to normally having it. I think my parents thought I was crazy, and I think they were a bit annoyed that I had never wanted to do housework or yard work at THEIR home. So be it. I would also catch some flak from my friends. One of my friends asked me how much Mr. Wilkens was paying me to mow his lawn. I said "nothing." My friend thought I was stupid and crazy for mowing his lawn for free. My friend said,

Why are you being stupid and mowing his lawn for free?"

My answer back was, "I am getting more in return than you can imagine."

Of course, my friend didn't accept that as a legitimate answer, but I didn't care. I just ignored everyone's criticisms. It seemed I had reached a point in my life where I figured out it was more important to do all the right things, rather than worry about what others said about what you did.

It wasn't all just work though. I actually had fun helping Mr. Wilkens. One day after I had mowed his grass, I came inside to cool off and rest. He would always have a drink and an ice cream treat waiting for me. All of a sudden we heard a commotion outside. We looked outside through the curtains and saw a couple neighborhood kids had pulled up onto his grass with their bicycles. I said to Mr. Wilkens, "Watch this!" Without missing a beat, I went to the front door, opened it, and yelled as loud as I could,

"GET OFF MY LAWN!"

The two kids were so startled and confused, they didn't know what to do, and they took off. When I shut the door, Mr. Wilkens and I burst out into hysterical laughter. Mr. Wilkens nearly spit out his tea and was laughing harder than I had ever seen him laugh in my life. He laughed so hard, there were tears coming out of his eyes. It took him about five minutes to calm himself. I am not sure what was more fun, yelling at those kids, or watching Mr. Wilkens's reaction. But it was the best!

Mr. Wilkens and I were having plenty of fun. I was having a great summer. I could have never imagined that I could have such a great summer mostly just doing chores. Who would have known! Certainly my parents were completely mystified. However, there was a certain feeling in the air that was kind of scary to me. Mr. Wilkens kept getting worse. It was clear to me where this was headed. To add to the anxiety, the school year was about to start back up again for the Fall. I wasn't sure how I would manage to look after Mr. Wilkens and go to school all day. I warned Mr. Wilkens that I would have to go back to school, but that I would check on him every day after school. He said I didn't have to, but at that point I knew he NEEDED and WANTED me to check on him.

When I was about to leave, he started to stumble around the kitchen counter looking for something. He found it and handed it to me. It was a key. He said that I should take a key to his door so that I could just come in. This way he would not have to answer the door every time. I told him I would keep it safe and not lose it. He said he knew.

Every day after school I stopped by to check on Mr. Wilkens. I would knock on the door once and then just let myself in with my key. I noticed he was often laying on the couch. He didn't seem to ever be up and walking around anymore. He even started asking me to bring him some soup or things he had in the kitchen. I wondered how he functioned all day alone. I did the best I could to help him. I took care of all his immediate requests after school, and then I would do all the house chores and lawn work on the weekend.

One evening when I got home, my mom said that she was proud of me for helping Mr. Wilkens. She said that if there was ever a moment that I needed help or something happened, that I should come to her, and she would help me. It was odd for her to say something like that, so I was disturbed by her comment because it felt ominous.

Mr. Wilkens continued to decline, but he still seemed like himself. He could still answer questions, he never lost his smile, and he could still laugh. However, I also received an ominous sign from him, similar to what I got from my mother.

One day Mr. Wilkens had the checkers and chess sets both sitting out. We hadn't been playing them because we simply did not have time anymore with all the chores. As I was about to leave his house to go home, he said to me,

"I want you to take the checkers and chess sets and hold onto them for me, Okay?"

My first instinct was to say no because they were his, not mine. They belonged with him. I always thought of them as being at HIS house. I identified those as being linked to Mr. Wilkens. Therefore, they should stay with Mr. Wilkens. However, he insisted. I said to him,

"Okay, but I will eventually bring them back here."

Mr. Wilkens just nodded his head in agreement. So, I took home the checkers and chess sets to keep in my room at home.

Not long after him giving me the checkers and chess sets, Mr. Wilkens asked me if there was anything else I saw in his house that I liked. It was an uncomfortable question for me. I also didn't have a good answer. But then it came to me. I sheepishly replied to him,

"I really love your military jacket in the closet. You know, the one with all the medals." I felt bad saying that, BUT HE ASKED. There was a long pause and almost a look of disappointment on his face. I immediately felt bad for saying the jacket. Before I could withdraw my request he said,

"I'm afraid that is the ONE thing I am going to need still."

I was confused by that answer and was just silent while I processed it. But then my thoughts turned dark and I figured out why he needed to keep it. This made me very upset, but I tried not to show it. I said to him, "After thinking about it, I think it's better you keep the jacket anyway."

I was trying to smooth it all out, but it was already awkward, and I was already upset at the thought of why he needed to keep it. I just changed the subject and hoped he would not ask me anymore questions about things I wanted in his house. He didn't bring things like that up again.

He continued to decline, and I was preparing myself for what might happen. It seemed Mr. Wilkens was doing the same. During one of my after-school visits, he said he wanted to have a little talk with me. He told me to have a seat in the chair he had moved next to the couch, since he was always taking up the entire couch now by lying on it.

I asked him what I could help him with. He started making what seemed like a prepared speech. He told me that his home meant everything to him and that he never wanted to leave his home. He said he wanted to make sure that nobody tried to take him out of his home. I kind of understood what he was getting at. I listened intently because I knew it was serious. He said that if he started to get really sick, or if something bad happened, that I should not call for help right away. He said that if I called for help, they would come and get him and take him away from his home. He said,

"I don't want anyone to take me away until I am gone."

I replied to him, "Sir, that does not make any sense."

He just stared at me. I said, "How can anyone take you away if you are already gone?"

He kept staring trying to understand what I had said, then he smiled and laughed. He then said,

"You are too smart for your own good." He tried again, and said, "If something bad happens to me, don't call for help until it's too late." He just stared, and I think he was afraid those blunt words might upset me, but they didn't. For some reason, I was able to handle the reality of his request.

I said, "Yes Sir, I understand."

It was a late Fall day and I was stopping by Mr. Wilkens's house after school. I used my key to enter, and he was laying on the couch. He seemed worse and more silent than usual. Usually he would at least look over at me as I was walking through the door. This time he didn't. I went over to him and it looked like he had been sleeping. He opened his eyes and tried to smile at me, but couldn't really. It was as if he did not even have the energy to smile.

I silently sat next to him in the chair. I pretended everything was okay and asked him how he was doing. He kind of grunted but didn't really answer. It was really uncomfortable and I was starting to get sad. I had never seen him like this before, and I had never been in a situation like this before. But then he asked for some water. I was relieved he said something, and wanted water. I went to get the water and brought it back to him. He motioned for me to leave it on the table. He didn't drink it.

I asked him again how he was doing. He was more responsive this time. His answer was, "I'm lucky." I didn't know what to say to that. Then he said something else. He said, "Thank you boy." He said, "You gave me more from life in the last year than I got in the last twenty." I felt to be silent, but I said, "Yes Sir." Then he was silent and I was silent. I don't think he had the strength to say anything, and I felt too awkward to say anything, and I didn't know the right thing to say.

After a few minutes of mutual contemplation and silence from both of us, he seemed to start moving or fussing a bit. He was trying to get his hand out from under the blanket or something. He was able to do this, and looked like he was kind of reaching toward me, but I was not sure. I instinctively said,

"Yes?" very softly.

Then he mumbled, "You are the very...."

He didn't finish the sentence. It just stopped there.

I kind of just silently waited to see if he would try again.

He didn't.

In fact, he didn't move at all after that.

I started to become upset. I think I knew. Finally, after what felt like an eternity, I got the courage to get up and go over and look at him more closely. I went over and looked at him. I will never forget it.

He was so peaceful, and looked like he was sleeping, except his eyes were open. There was nothing in the eyes. I knew right then. I guess I already knew, but I definitely knew when I saw his eyes.

I surprised myself by remaining calm. I kind of took a few steps away as if to think about what to do next. I glanced up at the pictures on his wall, and for some reason they made me start crying. My face was full of tears, I was confused, stunned, and not sure what to do, but I still remained calm.

For some reason I felt I needed to be sure. I went back over to him. I saw he was still motionless, and his eyes were still open without any life in them. For some reason I was kind of afraid to touch him, but I put the back of my hand right up to his mouth to see if I could feel any breathe.

I felt nothing.

I heard nothing.

Then I looked at his eyes again.

He was gone…

I remembered what he had told me about not wanting to be taken away from his house. So instead of panicking, I walked outside the house and sat on the front steps and started sobbing. I felt weird being inside the house with him dead. However, I also wasn't ready to leave yet. I sat outside thinking and crying.

The true weight of the loss hit me. I knew he was dead, but then I was hit with *HE IS GONE FOREVER*. This was a devastating thought. He was much of my world. He was my Grandpa, he was my friend, and he was my mentor in a way. How can I lose him and go on without him? My life will be empty without him. It's impossible, I can't just live on with him gone. I was starting to not even make sense with these thoughts in my head.

I calmed down and asked myself how long I should sit there doing nothing about this current situation. I remembered Mr. Wilkens said to wait until it was too late. For some reason I decided that about twenty minutes would be "too late," so there would be nothing they could do at that point. When I saw that about twenty minutes had passed, I decided I needed to go back into the house and check him one more time.

I went inside and calmly walked over to him. This time I was not as afraid, and I think I fully knew he was dead. Even so, I checked him anyways to make sure. His eyes were the same except more weird. It was obvious. The next thing I thought of was that I needed to go tell my mother. I knew this was the last time I would ever see Mr. Wilkens again. I stood over him. I stood over him like I was his grandchild. I stood over him like I was his son. I stood over him like I was a man. Then I had an idea. I knew what he wanted his military jacket for. I went to the closet and took the jacket out of the closet. I went back over to him and laid the jacket on top of him over his chest. I didn't want anyone to screw up and forget to put him in his jacket.

After laying his military jacket on him, I stepped back. I said, Thank you, Sir!" and I walked away.

I left the door to the house unlocked, and I left.

I calmly walked home and my mother was in the kitchen. I looked at her and started crying uncontrollably. She must have instantly figured it out. She held me. I finally got the voice to say "Mr. Wilkens is gone." My mom did not reply. She obviously figured that out. She just let me cry. When I was finished, I said, "No mom, really, Mr.

Wilkens just died and I don't know what to do." She then seemed a little startled and said, "Nobody is there?" I said "No, nobody knows, and he is dead." She got a little frantic and I said, "I left the door unlocked." I then saw my mom go to the telephone and she called the ambulance or police or somebody.

I didn't care.

It was over for me.

I just went to my room, closed the door, sat on my bed, and cried a little, and did lots of thinking.

I stared at the checkers and chess sets sitting there. Then I took the key to his house and put it in a little box. I didn't want to give it back to anyone. I was afraid someone would make me give it back. So I hid it in a box under my bed so I could keep it.

Eventually, I saw Mr. Wilkens's car disappear, then I saw it looked like his house was empty. Despite having a key, I never entered the house again. I stayed very quiet for a long time. My parents did not say much to me, and even everyone at school made sure not to say anything about Mr. Wilkens with me around. I was able to mourn in peace, and I did.

To this day, I still have the checkers and chess sets. I also still have the key to his house. I know Mr. Wilkens has his jacket. But what I have that is more precious than anything else, is that I have a Grandpa. Even though he is gone, I can still tell everyone that I had a Grandpa. I could never say that before I met Mr. Wilkens. But now, I always say I had a Grandpa. I don't bother telling anyone he was not my actual blood relative. I let them think he was related to me. I have all the stories I can tell about him. He was an amazing man. He was far more amazing than anyone in our neighborhood ever suspected or knew.

Thanks to Mr. Wilkens, I try to go through life looking to see the hidden true nature within people. The outer surface is usually not indicative of what's deep inside a person. Even with Mr. Wilkens, I think I only scratched the surface of what was really deep inside him. But for certain he was not just some grumpy old man who didn't like kids on his lawn. He was the most fascinating man I ever knew.

He also left me with a mystery that I will never solve. His final words to me. "You are the very."

I will never know what I am "very" of.

Very what?

I will never know.

I used to spend a lot of time sitting on the bench at the park trying to figure it out.

I finally realized that what was important is that I was "very" to him in some way.

He was "very" to me in many ways.

We should always try to be "very" in whatever we do, and be "very" in how well we treat others.

Mr. Wilkens was "very,"

and I am grateful he taught me to be the same.

CHAPTER THREE
The Silent Bully

Life is a patchwork of separate, but related stories, that intertwine to create the tapestry of our existence. I had my life at home with my parents, which was not much of a life. I had romances that tended to end in heartbreak. I had my relationships with friends that only survived for an allotted period of time. Then I had my own solitary life with myself, which was nearly all-consuming. However, there was one more portion of my life that cannot be ignored despite my desires to do so. School. I had my school life.

My school life could be divided into two main sections. First, there was the actual schoolwork. I was a pretty serious student, and I spent a lot of time and effort doing schoolwork and getting good grades. But the second and more consuming part of my school life was something I can only describe as DRAMA. And when I say drama, I don't mean the Drama Club where you get to put on school plays. When I say drama, I mean the social aspect of school that was always very complicated, difficult, and most often unpleasant.

I liked school (kind of), and I was somewhat social with friends, but I really despised the politics involved with school. What I mean by politics is which kids were popular, liked the most that particular day, hated the most that particular day, who was strongest, who was weakest, and so on. Every day at school was like entering a cage where there would be a fight to the death. Someone had to win and someone had to lose.

I do not know if it was like this in every school, or just more so at ours. Carlisle High School was a relatively small school in a small town, but we were all very competitive, and everyone wanted to be the best at something. We certainly did not want to be the worst at anything. Thus, there was this culture of pushing other kids down so that someone was always lower than you. The psychology was that even if you were not good at something, as long as there was another kid worse than you, it gave you some relief that you did not stick out as the worst.

You basically had a handful of kids who were the best at something, whether it be football, baseball, basketball, grades, intelligence, good looks, popularity, or whatever it was. There was always that lucky kid who happened to be the best in one or more of those areas. But then there were the rest of the kids, which was 99% of everyone. That last group had to fight amongst each other to not be the worst at something.

Usually, this created a battle between the kids who had the least going for them, and the kids who had the most vulnerabilities. So basically, you had the low-performing trouble-makers going after the kids who were the easiest targets to bully and make scapegoats.

Bullying was wide-spread. You could be bullied for anything, and usually everyone ended up being bullied for something. Obviously, the common themes were: too fat, too skinny, too poor, too rich, too smart, too dumb, too good looking, too ugly, and it went on and on. You couldn't win.

If you were poor, then you were looked down upon. But if you were rich, you were looked upon as too snooty. Most kids were either quite skinny or a bit husky. Both of those groups would get picked on. If you were seen as very good looking, you were considered an arrogant fake doll. If you were not super good looking, you were called ugly.

Smart kids were picked on for being too geeky, and kids who were not as smart were called stupid. So what level of intelligence was acceptable? Did anyone know? Was there a middle ground that was deemed as most desirable? Nobody knew. EVERYTHING was deemed as undesirable, and that left everyone open to being picked on in some fashion.

I was one of the lucky kids. I was not the best at anything, so I did not have the high level of scrutiny and constant challenges from other kids trying to steal the crown. But I also was not lacking heavily in any specific area, so I was not very vulnerable to attacks, and thus not an easy target for bullies. I was kind of in the upper middle, or lower top on a good day, of whatever it is we are talking about right now. So I guess you could say I had the privilege of blending in, remaining silent, and thus avoiding most of the bullying.

However, that is not to say I avoided bullying altogether. I did not. I had my share of problems. I came from a poor household, and thus I had clothes that were not the most stylish, nor did they always fit me correctly. I have to confess to perhaps being prepared for unexpected flooding at any moment, by the nature of my pants maybe being a bit too small for me, and riding up my ankles an inch or so too far.

I was also given a hard time because I did not have a stylish haircut like some of the other kids. Because we did not have much money, I grew up with my mother cutting my hair most of the time. I won't say that she used a bowl to cut my hair, but I will say that if she had used a bowl, my hair might have been cut more evenly than it was.

So, if a mean kid wanted to target me, they would certainly be able to find something about me that warranted being picked on. But other than that, I was of average height, decent enough appearance, no glasses, no obvious things wrong with me, and I did well in school. Like I said, I was one of the lucky ones. Most were not as lucky as me. Most were targeted by other kids in some way due to at least one glaring trait.

However, the kids at school were not the only problems when it came to this sort of toxic environment of bullying. Sometimes I felt as if the teachers participated as well. While the teachers never outright purposely tried to bully kids, there were times when I think the teachers could have done more to stop it. There were also times the teachers may have, without realizing it, instigated the environment for bullying.

One example of this was an incident I remember all too well involving one of my Advanced Placement English teachers and one of my fellow classmates, Jamie Winters. Jamie was a boy who had a stuttering problem. You might ask why a boy with a stuttering problem would be in an Advanced Placement English class with me. Well, despite Jamie's stuttering, he was an extremely talented writer. He excelled at both writing AND literature. He was definitely at an advanced level, and he definitely belonged in the advanced class. I considered Jamie to be the best creative writer in the entire class, including much more talented than myself, for sure. However, when it came to the "Speech" portion of the class, he obviously really struggled. He absolutely could not get through reading one paragraph, let alone one page or an entire essay, without completely breaking down into a stutter that left him "stuck," thus pretty much causing him to stop his presentation until he could get "unstuck."

For this reason, his "A" grades within Writing and Literature were always offset by a "D" grade in his Speech and Presentation units. Thus, Jamie would often end up with a "C" or "B-" at best as his English grade, even though he was definitely one of the best students in the class. This was so ridiculously unfair.

I'm not sure the teacher knew what to do with Jamie. I think Mr. Peker was conflicted as to whether Jamie belonged in the advanced class or not.

Oh yeah, did I mention our teacher's name was Mr. Peker?

Yes, that was his name.

A very unfortunate name for a high school teacher if you ask me.

His name was actually pronounced "Peeker" though. But I'm sure you can imagine for yourself how the kids actually pronounced his name when he was not around. Some of the kids called him "Mr. P," but that was not much better, and was just a continuation of the inside joke. His first name was Bill, and I always thought he would have been WAYYY better off just allowing us to call him Bill. But nope.

Oh, and get this. He had a son (who went to a different school), and his son's name was Richard, but everyone called him Dick. Seriously. Now, normally I don't see any problem with the name Dick, and I don't even think it's a funny name in any way. BUT, when your last name is Peker, I think it then becomes an issue, yes?

So, two questions. First off, his parents MUST have known what they were doing to the kid when they named him Richard, but called him Dick, right? And secondly, WHY would they name him that on purpose? Okay, wow, way off the subject now, but I am mentioning it because a teacher with the name Peker should certainly be extra sensitive to bullying, yes? I mean you can't tell me that Mr. Peker had not been bullied when he was a kid. I'm sure he was! Thus, he should be extra sensitive to it. But he wasn't!

One day Jamie Winters was standing up in front of the class TRYING to give a verbal presentation of an essay he had written. The essay was actually pretty good, but a little more than halfway through he totally lost his flow. As he always did, he fell victim to his stuttering and started doing so really badly.

For Jamie's part, he would always try really hard, and not give up. But sometimes the stutter would go on long enough where it would start to feel really uncomfortable and awkward. Some kids would just start laughing, but a lot of us like myself would just silently cringe and feel sorry for him. It would be easier if he would just stop, but he never did. He would keep trying until he could get beyond that *one* word or phrase he was hung up on. I think he knew that a horrible grade on a presentation would destroy his top grades in the other areas of the class, so it made him refuse to give up, which would have resulted in an "F."

I must say, I always thought Jamie had guts to stand up there and face what he must have known would be certain doom during these presentations. We ALL knew it was coming, and certainly Jamie knew it as well. However, he would stutter the same word like ten times if that is what it took to get unstuck and continue on so he could finish.

On this particular day, he got stuck during his presentation, and some of the kids started giggling. Then one kid in the class said out loud so everyone could hear,

"J J J J Jamie, t t t t try to f f f f finish."

A bunch of kids laughed. I looked over at Mr. Peker to see what he would do, and he did nothing.

He did not laugh, he did not smile, he did not acknowledge that the kids were laughing or taunting his stuttering,

BUT he was also not silencing them or yelling at them.

He just let it happen.

Just.

Let.

It.

Happen.

With his "silence."

I thought that was kind of mean and I almost wanted to say something to Mr. Peker like,

"Why are you letting them laugh and say those things?"

But Mr. Peker was the teacher and the authority figure, not me.

If I had said something to him, that could have been classified as being disrespectful to a teacher.

If the TEACHER, the AUTHORITY FIGURE, thinks this is okay, then who am I to speak up?

I need to just keep my mouth shut, right?

It was very uncomfortable though.

I never forgot about it, and I wondered about Mr. Peker after that. Did he hate Jamie for some reason? Did Mr. Peker want Jamie to get humiliated so that Jamie would leave the advanced class? Did Mr. Peker secretly think the stuttering was funny like some of the other kids? And another question.

How in the world did Jamie not break down crying and run out of the room? I would have.

Jamie just stood there and took it.

As if all of that was not bad enough, Mr. Peker started heckling Jamie, and kept asking him to repeat the entire sentence over and over again. He wouldn't let Jamie just get over the tough word and move on. He kept making Jamie start over and repeat the same sentence from the beginning until he got through it smoothly. But Jamie kept getting stuck on the same sentence.

It was so painful. I am speaking for myself, and I was not even the one getting humiliated in front of the class. I cannot imagine how awful this must have been for Jamie, yet Jamie just kept trying to do as

Mr. Peker was ordering him to do.

I am not sure if Mr. Peker was trying to help Jamie, or if Mr. Peker was annoyed that Jamie couldn't do the one sentence smoothly. Either way, it was torturous to watch, and inhumane to Jamie in my opinion.

The laughing in the class died down to simple boredom as everyone watched this play out way too long.

Finally, Mr. Peker said, "Never mind, just finish as you can." Jamie just skipped that one sentence and was able to finish the rest of his presentation quite smoothly.

His essay was one of the better ones in class, but he probably got an "F" or "D" on that presentation. Something felt very unfair about it all, but that was not my concern, I guess.

Unfortunately for Jamie, even after the humiliation of class had ended, he would then have to relive the entire experience in the hallways and outside of school when some of the kids would repeat everything that happened in school that day. Kids would walk past him and stutter certain words that Jamie had got stuck on that particular day in his various classes.

I would see this day after day because my locker was not far from his. He would be minding his own business, getting his books for his next class, and some kid would start stuttering as they were walking past him. It was really annoying. I did not find it funny at all, mostly because it was the same old crap every day. Even if it was funny, which it wasn't, the funniness ends after the 100th time it's done, you know what I mean? Just stop already, Ugh.

Every once in a while, Jamie would see that I was watching, and I would just kind of shrug, and maybe make some gesture indicating he should just forget about those guys saying that crap to him. But that was the only extent of my involvement. I was not about to confront those boys giving him a hard time. I had my own problems to contend with and didn't need any more. So I did nothing.

I did nothing about Jamie being bullied, just like I did nothing about everyone else being bullied. I was as silent bystander. I just stood there and watched it all, while doing nothing. I did nothing at all. And soon we would see the results of doing nothing at all.

One morning when I got to school, there was a very dark mood with everyone talking quietly to each other. I went to one of my friends and asked what was going on. What I was told would change my life forever.

Jamie Winters had killed himself.

That's it. Jamie was dead. It's something that takes your breath away. It's not just that someone died. It's that someone so young died. It's that someone you knew died. It's that the person died by killing themselves. It's just layer after layer after layer, one on top of the other. You begin to feel buried under it all.

I was not a friend of Jamie's really, but I knew him pretty well since we were in that English class together, and I had seen him around school all the time. More so, I had seen him being victimized on almost a daily basis. Jamie was kind of famous in our school. He was famous as being the kid who stuttered and got constantly bullied. So yeah, he was famous. But he was not famous for good reasons.

Were any of these reasons his fault? Was it his fault he stuttered? Was it his fault he got bullied all the time? NONE of this was his fault. Jamie was actually a nice kid. He was funny also. Jamie was a kid that would keep trying and never give up. He had humility. He knew he was not perfect, and he knew he would get picked on. He accepted this as his reality and still did the best he could.

I would never forget how Jamie REFUSED to give up in English class, despite constant hammering and criticism from the kids and even his teacher. What a disgrace, how we treated him. Listen to me saying all kinds of nice things about Jamie? Did I say those nice things about him while he was alive? Why not?

I hate it when someone dies and everyone just says all the nice things about them, and all their great memories, but in reality the person was treated like crap by everyone around them. I'm doing it now. I am one of those pathetic excuses for a human who treated Jamie like crap, but then says nice things about him after he is dead. I am pathetic.

Jamie was murdered in my opinion. He was murdered by everyone who ever bullied him. But guess what? He was also murdered by everyone who didn't bully him, but did NOTHING about the bullying. I was one of those. I never bullied him even once. But I also never stood up for him once. That makes me a bully also. I am a silent bully. I stay silent while I watch someone get bullied until he's dead. Does my silence make me any better than those who did the actual bullying? Am I not as bad as the person who bullies someone, just because I remain silent and don't sling any of the insults directly?

Why is silence considered innocence? If you sit in silence while others are being victimized, how does that make you not guilty? Why is it okay to be silent? And why was I so silent? Did I not care what happened to Jamie? Did I gain any entertainment from watching the festivities? Or was I just afraid to get involved? Was I afraid I would be bullied also?

Is it easier to watch someone else die than it is to face the problems that might come from getting involved? Why do we just remain silent when we see something going on that is not right? Why do we watch others suffer, and do nothing? It all made me feel like a useless piece of garbage as a person.

While I processed my shock, horror, anger, and disgust within myself, I learned more details that made it even worse. How could this get any worse, one might ask? Well, the details of his suicide started to leak out amongst the students and spread like wildfire.

It was after school hours when it was dark and nobody was there, that Jamie was found by the school janitor hanging from a tree near the gymnasium. The janitor, Mr. Fiske, noticed that the supply closet in the gym was open. He saw that the long ladder was missing. He peaked outside the gym doors just to see if someone had dragged the ladder outside as a prank of some sort. When he looked out, he saw the ladder fallen over on the grass, and then he saw Jamie Winters hanging by a rope from a tree branch.

The story goes that Mr. Fiske managed to cut Jamie down in less than a minute, but it was way too late. Jamie had likely been hanging from that tree for over an hour. Jamie had managed to rig the rope around the tree, then climb the ladder, tie the rope around his neck, and I guess kicked the ladder out from under him so it would fall over. I don't want to think about what happened after that.

I also don't want to think about what it must have been like for Mr. Fiske to find Jamie. The rumor was that Mr. Fiske was too upset to return to school. There were rumors that the entire tree was going to be cut down, and other rumors of what Jamie was wearing, and so on it went with all the many rumors.

One rumor that turned out to be verified as true immediately, was that Jamie had written a note and it was found sticking halfway out of his pants pocket after he was cut down from the tree.

The note read, *"You all wanted me dead so I fixed the problem."*

Yes, that's what the note said. That is all it said.

Was that clear enough for everyone?

Did it need to be any clearer?

Should he have written more?

Did he need to say more?

The answer is "No!"

Jamie was right to feel how he did, and we all knew what we had done to him, or not done by remaining silent. He just said bluntly what the painful facts were.

Look how he was treated?

If you look at it from his point of view, it would appear true that nobody wanted him alive.

Who would treat someone so badly unless they wanted them not around anymore?

And all of this just because he stuttered?

REALLY??

People made him feel like everyone wanted him dead just because he had a stuttering problem? Or was it more? Was it maybe that picking on Jamie for his stuttering, made weaker kids feel more powerful. Maybe making Jamie miserable made other kids feel better about their own miserable lives.

It just seemed all so pointless.

Jamie was a nice kid who stuttered.

That's it.

End of story.

End of Jamie's story.

But it was not the end of my story about Jamie. I now had an anger and guilt I could not shake for even five minutes. I was furious. Other kids were pretending they were his friend and crying, even though they were not his friend. The other kids who actively bullied him just remained silent and tried to blend in with the surroundings as if they were invisible and nothing had happened. The irony was thick. Those who bullied became silent, and those who were silent were now speaking. I think I was the only one who was ANGRY. I was FURIOUS. But furious at what? Was I furious at what happened to Jamie? Furious at other kids for what they did to Jamie? Or was I furious at MYSELF for doing NOTHING?

My subsequent soul-searching would determine it was the latter. The last one. My anger eventually turned mostly to guilt, and my guilt took root inside me like a hundred-year-old tree affixed to the Earth's core.

After my guilt had been consuming me for many weeks, I really couldn't handle it anymore. I knew what happened to Jamie was not my fault DIRECTLY, but I still felt that MAYBE I could have avoided it from happening if I had done more, or done *something* different.

Ironically, the other kids who WERE actually more directly responsible, didn't seem to want to think about it or take responsibility in any way. They never spoke of Jamie, and just wanted to wipe the entire incident from their minds. How could they deal with it so easily, while I was being EATEN ALIVE with guilt?

I was lying in bed trying to fall asleep one night, and I suddenly sat up and realized what I had to do. The pain of dealing with this silently within myself was unbearable. I felt I had been a coward for not speaking up in defense of Jamie when he was being bullied.

I WAS TIRED OF BEING A COWARD.

I wasn't going to do it anymore.

I knew what I had to do.

I had to take full responsibility for my part, and have the courage to fully own it, and face my consequences like a man, instead of a coward who stays in silence and lets others suffer. I decided I was going to do the most scary, worst possible, most uncomfortable, and possibly very inappropriate thing possible.

I NEEDED to go see Jamie's parents. I needed to tell them the truth. I needed to apologize. I needed to let them hate me or do whatever they wanted to do to me. I didn't care anymore. The pain of guilt was much worse than the fear of facing Jamie's parents.

The next day after school I nervously walked over to Jamie's house. As I walked up to the front door I could feel my throat closing up. My breathing got tight and I was sweating. I was scared to death, I really was. But I was done being a coward.

I knocked on the door. Jamie's mother answered. She looked surprised to see me, and of course she had no idea who I was, since I had never been to Jamie's house before. She asked what she could do for me. I explained to her that I was sort of a friend of Jamie's (lie), and I wondered if it would be okay if I talked to her about something. She seemed concerned and intrigued at the same time, and motioned me to come inside.

Jamie's father was sitting at the dining room table. It looked like maybe I had interrupted them having coffee or dinner or something. But there was no stopping now. Jamie's mom told me to have a seat at the dining room table with them. Jamie's mom looked at the dad and just said, "This young man says he has something to say about Jamie." That got the father's attention and they both just stared at me.

Now only if I could get my voice to work. I almost forgot what I was going to say with all the stress. It felt very intimidating. The mom broke the awkward moment and asked if I could tell them who I was. I told them my name. Their reaction was such that I felt they had heard of me and knew who I was. This only made me more nervous. I wondered if maybe Jamie had said something horrible about me.

The father then said, "So what would you like to tell us young man?" With that invitation, I just let all of it spill out like a dam finally breaking after holding back an entire lake of water. I had weeks of guilt and pain stored up, and it all was in the process of flowing out. I told them everything, including things that were not relevant. I told them how I had seen Jamie getting bullied numerous times, and that I did NOTHING. I told them that I never once said anything mean to Jamie, but I also never did anything to stop those that did.

I told them that I was so sorry. I told them that it could be my fault and I'm so sorry. I had started crying not long after my confessional rant had started, but I was crying even harder now. They knew I was done and had nothing left when I just kept saying "I'm sorry" over and over again. The mom got me some tissues. I could barely breathe I was so upset, and I was practically convulsing gasping for breaths. I noticed the mom was also crying and the father's eyes were all red.

I wasn't sure if they might kill me now. I was awaiting my fate while also trying to get control of myself and wipe all the tears from my face. When I had calmed down a bit, the mom came over and put her hand on my shoulder and said, "We don't blame you for Jamie's death my dear."

Then the dad spoke up and said,

"We know it's not your fault young man."

I started to speak and say, "Yes, but..," however the father interrupted me.

He said, "Jamie left us a longer note in his bedroom."

This was news to me and made me completely silent. The father said, "Jamie wrote down the names of all the kids who he felt bullied him." "Your name wasn't on it."

I felt a HUGE sense of relief with this news. I honestly felt it could have gone either way, and maybe Jamie could have been so mad that he added my name to the list.

The father then said, "Jamie also wrote down a list of who he wished he had become better friends with."

He paused, and then he said, "Your name was the only one he listed."

I was stunned by this. They must have seen the shock on my face. I didn't remember having very many positive interactions with Jamie. I mostly just didn't have negative ones. I basically had "nothing ones." I was surprised he would have liked me enough to want to be friends with me.

I had nothing in me to say except,

"I had no idea Jamie wanted to be friends."

They both looked at me kind of lovingly and said,

"Jamie must have seen something within you that he liked."

I had no reply for that, so I said nothing.

All I could think of to say during the awkward silence was, "I'm still really sorry, I should have helped him."

His father got up from the table and said, "Young man, I respect you a great deal for coming over here to talk with us, and your honesty." The father continued, "I would have been very pleased to have you as my son's friend."

At that point, the mother also got up from the table. I knew it was time for me to go. I didn't feel I had said everything I wanted to say, but all I could think of was, "I'm sorry," and frankly I think they were tired of hearing it over and over from me. So I got up and started toward the door. I looked at both of them and said,

"I won't make this mistake again." Jamie's dad looked at me and said,

"I believe you son."

With that, I left and went home. I was totally drained, but I slept well for the first time since Jamie's death.

I took it as a sign that Jamie was okay with me now, and would let me have some peace. Hopefully Jamie could have some peace also.

After Jamie's death, my battle with guilt, and my visit to Jamie's parents, I was kind of a new person. I would no longer be a silent bully by allowing things to happen, and I would no longer be a coward. It was not long before this new philosophy and way of life for me would be put to the test.

Appropriately, the first major test happened in the same environment in which I had failed so miserably in the past. It happened in Mr. Peker's English class. We were in the Literature unit of the class, and we were supposed to have read a certain book and were discussing it in class.

Mr. Peker liked to call upon a variety of people, hoping to "catch them" as having not done the homework or read the assigned book. If he KNEW you read the book and did the work, he would never call on you. But if he smelled blood in the water and thought maybe you didn't do the work, he would DEFINITELY call on you. And if you someone who managed to evade his first question, he would call on you again, knowing the second time might be the charm and he would catch you as having not done the assignment.

Mr. Peker didn't like me much, but he didn't dislike me either. He knew I always did the assignments, and I usually got a good grade on my assignments. Therefore, he almost never called on me. So that part was good, and he thought I was a solid student. However, he thought my writing was crap. He might have been right about that, but you should still motivate your students in a different way rather than just letting them know their writing is crap.

I had a very informal writing style. I liked to write so that people felt I was talking with them personally. I wanted my writing to be very relatable, easy, and comfortable for my reader. However, Mr. Peker thought of this style of writing as something belonging in a garbage dumpster.

Mr. Peker was a fan of Shakespeare, and I was NOT Shakespeare, nor did I want to be. Instead of using classical tautological, potentially superfluous pros, I preferred using slang and phrasing more representative of how people actually spoke in real life. Therefore, my writing was garbage to him, and I am certain he would still feel the same today. Regardless, I always did the assignments as instructed, and thus he HAD to score my work decently.

But anyway, there was this kid in my class on this one particular day that obviously had not done the homework. He was a pretty good student, thus why he was in the advanced class, BUT this kid always had a job outside of school. There were times he would work really late, then come home and go to bed. He simply did not have time for homework sometimes. All of us kids knew this. He would sometimes not do well on tests, but we knew it was only because he was always working his job. He was a really smart kid, and if he DID study, he always got an "A."

On this day, I think Mr. Peker was in a bad mood, and he was out for blood. He could smell blood in the water, and knew this kid didn't read the book the night before. He called on this kid to give details on one of the chapters. The kid tried to fake it and give some details that he already knew about the general story. But Mr. Peker wasn't buying it. Mr. Peker kept narrowing in with more specific questions to him. The kid finally gave up and just started to say, "I'm not sure, I don't know." Mr. Peker, being annoyed, just kept asking questions. Mr. Peker was firing off one question after another even though the kid already admitted he didn't know any of the answers.

It started to become uncomfortable, and I started to get that same cringe-like feeling that I had experienced during the instances with Jamie Winters. Something inside me got triggered and ignited. It only took me 3.2 seconds to automatically react without fully thinking through my actions or consequences. I surprised myself and all of a sudden erupted OUT LOUD, VERY LOUDLY,

"Mr. Peker, he already said he doesn't know, leave him alone!"

Everyone in the room, including myself, were shocked at my outburst and you could hear a pin drop as everyone, including Mr. Peker, looked over at me.

I knew I had already "done it" and was screwed, so I decided to dig all the way in. I just stayed motionless and stared him down like I was not backing down.

Mr. Peker then said to me,

"You think it's a problem that I push my students to do better?"

Without any hesitation I replied, "Oh, like you tried to make Jamie Winters better by pushing him?"

There were audible gasps in the room. I don't think anyone had even said the words "Jamie Winters" out loud in a classroom since his death.

Mr. Peker just stared at me like a deer in headlights. All he said was, "Please leave the classroom, I think you need a break." I just stared back at him while simultaneously packing up my stuff and walking out of the classroom.

It was not unnoticed by me that Mr. Peker had not actually sent me to the principal's office. He just sent me out of the classroom. I'm assuming he didn't send me to the office because he KNEW I was right, and he dared not escalate this matter to higher powers. After the class, some of the kids showed their approval that I had the balls to stand up to Mr. Peker. I don't think they cared that it was about defending a fellow student, or about bullying. They were just impressed I was not scared to confront a teacher.

As for Mr. Peker, he never mentioned anything to me about it, and he never paid me much attention at all after that. He just let me silently glide smoothly through his class. Furthermore, I think I had unintentionally also sent a message to all the kids in school that I was not afraid to speak up or confront anyone on things I didn't like. I became the kid who bullies left alone.

The rest of my year went pretty smoothly after that. I never personally got bullied for anything again. However, there were times when I would walk up on incidences of kids picking on other kids. Whenever this happened, I would immediately intervene and attempt to stop it. It is possible I became a little overly enthusiastic about my new-found attitude though.

One day out on the school grounds, I walked up on an interaction where one of the known trouble-maker kids was making fun of this other kid. The kid being picked on was a bit over weight, short, and wore glasses. He was a prime target. The mean kid was calling him fat and four-eyes, and all kinds of things. I got closer and said, "Just leave him alone."

The mean kid then said to me, "Oh you want to mess with ME, Mr. Hero?"

`I said, "No, I just want you to leave him alone."

`The mean kid walked over to me and said, "How about I mess with you instead then?"

`I kind of sighed. I obviously didn't want to get into a fight, and especially with some nasty trouble-maker kid bigger than me. However, I was firmly settled into my new "not a coward" personality.

I just stood there not backing down and said, "just leave him alone."

The mean kid responded by pushing me so that I almost fell over backwards. Something inside me snapped. I was okay with insults, words, threats, and that kind of thing, but APPARENTLY I was NOT okay with anyone pushing me. I know this because my immediate automatic response was to punch the kid in the stomach with the force of a super-human. It was so violent, that I scared myself, and the kid was incredibly stunned as well. His response was to double-over and puke all over his shoes. It seemed like he was trying to puke while simultaneously catching his breath and not fall over dead. I was shocked, he was shocked, and the kid being picked on was shocked. *I really did not mean to do that.* It was so gross, I could actually see what he ate for lunch. He had clearly had the corn chowder, and I'll leave it at that. I think all of us were really grossed out.

The kid being picked on ran off because it was just too gross and too scary to hang around. The mean kid was sick and in pain from what had just happened, and I was HORRIFIED at what just happened. I didn't mean to hurt him. I just wanted him to back away and not touch me. Out of some weird backwards instinct, I apologized to the kid. I told him I was "sorry," and that I didn't mean to hurt him like that. Of course, this was an ironic thing for me to say, because if you played back what happened in your mind, you could see I hit this kid in the stomach with so much force that anyone would assume I was trying to hurt him, if not kill him. But honestly, I didn't realize my own strength or something. I didn't mean to do that. Hitting him and seeing him puke was disturbing to me for some reason. I was genuinely sorry.

More odd, was how I kept telling him I was sorry even though it was HIM who had provoked the entire incident. I think he was confused as to what to say and what to do. I suppose part of him wanted to run away, and part of him wanted to kill me. For my part, I walked closer to him and patted him on the shoulders in a friendly way, and said again I was sorry and didn't mean to hurt him. He just looked at me like I was an alien with super powers and said,

"Yeah whatever, it's fine."

I asked him if he was going to be okay, he nodded, and I then walked off.

Most would have viewed this incident as a huge victory for me, and against bullying. Some would think this might have made me "king of the jail yard." But no. The three of us involved never spoke of the incident, so nobody knew. For me, I was ashamed at what I had done. I had turned into the same kind of violent kid that I didn't like. Similar to how when I realized I had been a "silent bully," I felt that maybe I was being the problem. I was realizing that I had turned into a violent kid who got into fights and hurt people. This was NOT who I was, or who I wanted to be.

After this incident, I dialed it down a bit and never hit another person again for the rest of the school year, and in fact never hit another person again in my life. Violence is not the answer any more than bullying is. It's hard to learn balance in life I guess, but I was giving it a good effort. I spent the rest of the school year being someone who was never afraid of anyone, never afraid to speak up, but someone who believed in resolving problems without any violence if at all possible. I was teaching myself, I was learning, and unknowingly I was teaching others by example. I may not have been the smartest kid, best looking kid, or most popular kid, but I was the most respected kid. I'll take that.

I remember spending time sitting on the bench at the park after school thinking about all I had learned about myself and others. It dawned on me that EVERYONE had some kind of vulnerability that left them open to being picked on. Whether it was their weight, height, voice, accent, glasses, clothes, haircut, stutter, last name, or medical problem. Or whether they were poor, rich, smart, not so smart, and tons of other things I could list. Everyone has something.

I wondered why people throw stones in glass houses, because by definition, the bully would also have things about themselves that leave them open to bullying. So if they might be bullied, then why are they bullying others. I guessed the answer was that they might be bullying others as a way of taking attention away from themselves so that they wouldn't get bullied. I know there is more to it than that though, and later understood that bullies bully because they are in pain about something in their own lives. Bullies bully, and bullies get bullied. Why do people even bother with this game? Everyone loses eventually.

These were just examples of some thoughts I would have while sitting at the park contemplating life. I was becoming an adult, even though I felt I had already become a man long ago. It was time for me to wrap up my high school years, and move on to see what life would have in store for me next.

One of the many events that were a part of finishing up my final year in high school, was the school assembly where scholarship awards were announced and given out. I had to endure this boring assembly each and every year as an underclassman, but this year I would finally be part of the senior class who were actually receiving the awards.

This was a tense event for some of us because our hopes of going to college often rested upon whether we received some sort of scholarship or not. Or I should say, it was a tense time for those of us who came from families without money. Those families with plenty of money could easily proceed with any secondary school plans they wanted without having to worry whether or not they would receive a scholarship award. As for me, I NEEDED a scholarship in order for me to proceed. With that said, I honestly was not that concerned about not getting a scholarship. Fortunately, our school had a program called the "Carlisle Scholarship."

A Carlisle Scholarship was usually awarded to ALL Carlisle High

School students who could demonstrate a financial need, had fairly decent grades, and had a desire or plans for secondary schooling. I checked all those boxes, and thus was pretty certain I would receive one of the scholarships. I believe my parents had the same assumption that I would qualify and receive this scholarship as well. We had filled out all the paperwork, submitted the application, and I was an "A" student on top of that. The Carlisle Scholarship paid for your first year of pretty much any college or university of your choice, other than the top Ivy League schools. Since I was looking at going to a state university somewhere, I knew I would be covered for my first year of schooling at the very least.

Despite my constant self-assurances that I was a shoo-in for the scholarship, I was still very anxious to be officially awarded it so that I would know that piece of business was all set, and I could put my mind at ease. My wait was about to be over because we had all filed into the gymnasium bleachers for the announcements, and Principal Bowman was at the microphone to begin. There was a lot of blah blah blah first about what a great school year it was and so forth, but he finally got down to it. He said he would call out all the names of the Carlisle Scholarship recipients for that year. In a way, these would be names of kids who did not have much money, but there was no shame in it because they were also names of everyone who had received very good grades and wanted to go to college.

Mr. Bowman started in on the names, and it seemed to go on for a while. I just stared at my shoes, carefully listening for my name. I felt my head was down for quite a long time when I heard him say,

"So those are all our Carlisle Scholarship recipients for this year, and we congratulate them all."

I almost felt like I needed to clean my ears out or something. I didn't hear my name! How could I not hear my name? I had that horrible feeling you get in the pit of your stomach when someone rejects you for something you were certain would go well. I felt my entire body go flush and I thought for a moment I might even faint. I looked over to my friend sitting next to me and asked if they had heard my name for the scholarship. Without missing a beat, they just nodded no.

I was devastated.

I didn't hear the rest of the assembly announcements because I trapped within my own mind of devastation. I just wanted to go home and cry.

I'm not sure what was more upsetting; the fact I was REJECTED for something I felt I definitely deserved, or the fact I was not going to have the money to start secondary school. I felt I had been punched in the gut and had the air knocked out of me.

All kinds of thoughts went through my head about possible reasons of why they decided to deny me.

Did it have something to do with things that happened at school that year?

Did one of the teachers I had issues with somehow block it?

Did I do something terribly wrong that I did not realize?

Did they just hate me?

Or maybe a supernatural force just wanted to ruin my life?

Whatever it was, I was screwed.

When we were released from that horrible nightmare of my life destruction, I went straight home. I went to my room and finally had the private cry that I had been dying for all afternoon after barely holding it in for so long. I felt like I had been totally forsaken, none of my hard work and good grades recognized, and that I had just been condemned to a life of failure and misery.

I realized that I had to tell my mother the news. She needed to know that I was a loser and my life was over. She was my mother after all, and despite us not always getting along, she deserved to know that I was doomed to a life of hopeless despair. I went down to the kitchen where she was calmly making dinner. She looked over at me, saw I was upset, and asked me what was wrong. I told her my dreams were dead because somehow I didn't get the scholarship.

Without even flinching my mother just said,

"Hmmm, well did you talk to Mr. Bowman about it?"

This is the ONE reply I was NOT expecting from my mother. She didn't act alarmed, AND she was suggesting I go crying to the principal about it?? First of all, I had NEVER even spoken to Mr. Bowman once during my entire time in school. Secondly, why was I going to further embarrass myself by crying to Mr. Bowman about my failure to be worthy of the scholarship that almost everyone with half a brain received?

So, I felt I needed to repeat it to my mother. I said to her,

"Mom, I won't be able to pay for my first year of school now."

Again, my mom just calmly said, "Perhaps you should speak with Mr. Bowman."

Again, shocked that my mother didn't seem to care that my life was ruined and over, I just gave up and went back up to my room. Had the entire world gone mad? I was totally rejected from a scholarship that I was a shoo-in for, and my mother didn't even care. Nobody cared. It was a bit confusing on top of being over-the-top distressing. I went to bed that night in some of the worst despair I had felt in a long time.

The next morning, I went to school as normal and felt like an emotionless zombie. I guess I was going to finish out all of my obligations with school, but had no interest in engaging in any more end-of-year celebrations, or even socializing with my friends. I figured I had better start figuring out what I was going to do with the rest of my sorry life.

I settled into my desk at my first period class, and was sulking and not even paying attention. However, I noticed the school secretary walk into the classroom and give the teacher a note. Whenever this happened, it usually meant that some kid was in big trouble and was being summoned to the principal's office for being a troublemaker.

The teacher glanced at the note, then looked up at me, and motioned for me to come forth. I was thinking, ME?? Certainly she was not pointing at ME! I sincerely thought it was a mistake and she must have been pointing at a kid in back of me or something, therefore I didn't move. But then she did it again, but this time said,

"NOW!"

I responded to her by pointing at myself as if to ask if she was seriously referring to me. She nodded in the affirmative. All the other kids whipped their heads around in shock and were all staring at me in amazement. I had NEVER gotten sent to the principal's office EVER, and everyone knew it.

I started shaking with nervousness and shock. I gathered my stuff up off my desk, nearly dropping everything all over the floor twice in the process because my hands were trembling. I walked up to the teacher, and she handed me the note and pointed to the door. I left the classroom shaking and barely able to breathe. I started to wonder if this was somehow a continuation of the nightmare from yesterday when I was overlooked for the scholarship. I began to wonder if I had somehow been sucked into a vortex and thrown into an alternate reality where I was one of the horrible kids. Or maybe I had somehow died and was in hell and didn't realize it yet. For whatever reason, my life had taken a very nasty turn for the worse, and perhaps the next stop would be doing hard time in prison for something I had no idea what I did.

I found my way to the principal's office, and I admit I was unsure of the way there because I had only been in that general area maybe twice before to see my guidance counselor. I walked up to the secretary's desk and just handed her the note. She looked at me slightly confused because I could tell she knew I had never been there before. She went into Mr. Bowman's office to tell him I was there, and then she came back out.

I had sat down in one of the "chairs of shame" while I was waiting. This was where all the bad kids sat, and now I was sitting there. My palms were sweaty and I was not certain I would be able to speak to Mr. Bowman without crying or passing out. The secretary came out and blandly said, "You can go right in." I felt like being super polite and saying thank you to her, but realized I should just shut up and do as I'm told without delay or talk-back.

I walked into Mr. Bowman's office, and he looked up at me. He immediately stood up from his desk and offered his hand to shake my hand. He said,

"Hey there, I'm Mr. Bowman, I don't think we have met yet."

I shook his hand with my sweaty clammy hand, for which he must have thought I had just been handling a dead fish or something, but he said nothing. I politely replied,

"Hi Sir, no Sir, we have never met."

He casually sat back down and motioned for me to take a seat in one of the chairs in front of his desk so that I could further sweat and tremble more. He said to me,

"I have heard plenty about you, and my only regret is that I never had a chance to meet you until now." He said it like we were at a neighborhood picnic or something. From his friendly laid-back mood toward me, I half expected him to make himself a drink and offer me one as well. It was weird.

My absolute terror turned to absolute confusion. I was now certain I had indeed been sucked up into a vortex and transported into an alternate reality. Mr. Bowman asked me,

"So, how are things going for you during these last days of your high school experience?"

Again, I was surprised and confused.

Why was he asking? Why did he care?

The truth is that this was officially the lowest point in my high school "experience."

I didn't answer right away, and Mr. Bowman just kept looking at me as if he seriously expected an actual reply.

Realizing it was possible that I was not about to be sentenced to a death sentence for some unknown crime I didn't commit, I made a flash decision in my head to be honest with him.

I replied, "Well, to be honest Sir, it's been rough."

Mr. Bowman looked extremely surprised and perplexed by my reply. He asked me why it was rough. I said to him,

"Well, I was kind of expecting and needing one of the Carlisle Scholarships so I could go to school, and I guess I was rejected for some reason."

Mr. Bowman's reaction was even more perplexing to me. He kind of smiled, paused, and started fiddling with things on his desk. It was clear to me that he either knew of this debacle, or he was amused by it, or perhaps both. He then looked up at me and said,

"Well there is a very good reason you were not awarded a Carlisle Scholarship." With that, he just looked at me squarely in the eyes and acted like that was all he was going to say. I couldn't help myself and said,

"Well I thought I had earned it, qualified for it, and deserved it." Mr. Bowman immediately replied,

"Yes you did, absolutely."

So I replied, "Then why didn't I get it?"

Notice that I stopped saying "Sir." I was no longer nervous, and at this point I was talking to him like an adult, and I seriously wanted answers. I was finally sticking up for myself instead of trembling like a coward. Whatever happened from this meeting, I would at least make my feelings known, and make him give me some answers.

Mr. Bowman stopped fiddling with things on his desk, but never stopped smiling. He looked at me and said,

"Did you know Henry Wilkens?" Stunned, I paused and replied, "Yeah, Mr. Wilkens was my Grandpa; I mean he wasn't my actual

Grandpa, but he was." Mr. Bowman looked at me like he was wondering if I was truly as intelligent as he had heard, but then said,

Well, when Henry Wilkens, excuse me, Mr. Wilkens, passed away, he left with the school trustees to hold, among other things, a scholarship specifically for you."

I heard every word Mr. Bowman had just said, but I couldn't believe what I had just heard, so I instinctually played dumb and said,

"What do you mean he left me a scholarship?" Mr. Bowman, by now probably thinking I was not very bright after all, said,

"The reason you didn't receive a Carlisle Scholarship is because Mr. Wilkens has left you a full four-year scholarship to the college or university of your choice." He continued, "We could not announce this at the school assembly because it was the wish of Mr. Wilkens that it remain anonymous, except to you obviously."

I was just trying to take all this in. I felt I could possibly faint, but at least this time it was for something good. I felt I needed to confirm what I heard, so I repeated and said to Mr. Bowman,

"So Mr. Wilkens left ME a full scholarship for all four years to whatever school I want to go to?" Mr. Bowman nodded and said,

Yep, I think you got it now son." But then he acted like he just remembered something else and he said,

"But that's not all."

I said, "Why, what else?"

Mr. Bowman said, "He has also left you a very substantial travel stipend for any traveling you wish to do until those funds are exhausted."

This time I was the one who smiled. While Mr. Bowman himself seemed perplexed by the travel stipend, I totally understood it. Mr. Wilkens was a world traveler, and he knew that I was very intrigued by all of his travels. It made total sense to me that Mr. Wilkens might help me do some traveling.

However, I still had questions as I was processing all of this news. I said to Mr. Bowman,

"You said something about 'among other things'. What did you mean about 'among other things?'"

Mr. Bowman said, "Oh, well in addition to YOUR scholarship, he funded a program where we can provide financial assistance to those students needing it, to go on our yearly school trip overseas." I let that sink in and process in my mind. Then I said,

"OHHHHHH, so like when Jamie Winters got to go on the school trip to Paris." Mr. Bowman not wanting to divulge personal financial information about the Winters I suppose, just shook his head in the affirmative and said,

"Yeah like that."

I then said, "Wow1"

Mr. Bowman replied with, "Wow indeed."

Then Mr. Bowman quickly added, "There is one more thing I would like to tell you."

I said, "Yeah, what's that?"

Mr. Bowman then said, "Mr. Wilkens in his award letter to the school, said that it was specifically because of you, young man, that he was inspired to donate to our travel program." He continued on, "I am not sure what you did to impress him, but he saw something in you that inspired him to help our kids for many years into the future, and as the principal, I would like to thank you, young man."

I just shook my head, not knowing what to do or say, and said, "Well, let's just thank Mr. Wilkens." Mr. Bowman replied,

"Okay son, as you wish." He then looked like he was late for something, and all of a sudden I noticed people stacking up in the hallway waiting to see him. I had gotten totally lost in this exchange and was not sure if ten minutes had passed or ten hours. I snapped back into reality, stood up, and said,

"Thank you Sir."

Mr. Bowman said, "No. Thank YOU. SIR."

With that, we both smiled at each other and I walked out. The secretary looked at me inquisitively as if to wonder why I was in there for so long, had apparently had not been put to death, and I was even smiling.

I pulled myself together and figured out I needed to rush to my second period class, and I did. And with that, all was right with the world again. I spent the rest of the day playing out everything again in my head. I realized that my mom must have known about all this, and that is why she never panicked, and told me to talk to Mr. Bowman. I wondered how long my mother knew about all this, and who told her. I wondered what Mr. Bowman must have been thinking about me these past years, knowing all along I had this scholarship waiting for me. It was like I had been living my life without knowing my true reality these past years. How bizarre I had gone through my high school years thinking I was a struggling underdog who might not make it, but in reality I was probably the most privileged kid in school the entire time.

After school, I went to the park and sat on the bench. I thought about the entire situation, still trying to grasp what had just happened. I thought Mr. Wilkens just wanted me to have the chess set and checkers set. I thought that was the end of it. But come to think of it, I didn't think he had much family, and perhaps if I had been older at the time I might have wondered about this kind of stuff. But I just never thought of it. Mr. Wilkens went through a lot of effort to make sure I would be okay. It brought some old feelings back and I started to tear up thinking of him. It was like after all this time of him being gone, he was still here. He was still having a huge influence on my life, even now. What an incredibly smart amazing man. What an incredibly GENEROUS man. And the other thing, is that some of these kids who used to make fun of Mr. Wilkens and taunted him, had likely been the same kids who benefited from his generosity and got to travel the world thanks only to Mr. Wilkens.

I would love to have told some of those snots that the man they thought was mean, was the only reason they were able to go on the school trip. However, I decided to honor what Mr. Bowman said about keeping that anonymous. Still, I felt a tremendous amount of satisfaction knowing that in a way Mr. Wilkens got the last laugh by helping these snotty kids who didn't even realize all this, and that the "grumpy old man" made their traveling possible.

As for Jamie Winters, it felt so right that Mr. Wilkens, the kindest man I ever met, would have had a hand in providing Jamie one of his few joyful victories in life. Jamie was so proud and happy that he got to go on that Paris trip. Nobody knew how he and his family could afford it, and Jamie never said a word. But now I knew. Mr. Wilkens would have been pleased about helping Jamie.

Even more so, I hoped that Mr. Wilkens would be proud of me. I had made my mistakes, but I did my very best to own those mistakes, and turn myself into a better person. I did my best to turn into a person that Mr. Wilkens would be proud of. I don't know if I fully succeeded, but I know I had done my best.

After graduation, I remember sitting on the park bench being thankful for Mr. Wilkens providing me with my secondary education and chance to travel the world; and being thankful for Jamie Winters, who forced me to become a man of independent integrity instead of a coward. I had plenty of others who had made me who I was as well, but I knew from there on out, it would be up to me to make myself whatever and whoever I decided to be.

CHAPTER FOUR
The Love Story

We are taking a trip way back in time, to a time long ago, when there was a beautiful young lady of barely eighteen years old named Beatrice. People called her Bea. She lived in a very small town with her parents. It was the kind of town that only had several houses scattered down each street, and was sustained only by a corner grocery store, and a bakery/cookie store that was owned by Bea's parents.

Bea worked for her parents in the bakery with her friend Maggie. It was a pretty routine and easy life, except during Christmas time when the bakery turned into a full-fledged cookie factory that produced all kinds of Christmas treats that would be sold as Christmas trays and platters to people in town, but additionally to nearby towns, and even large businesses in the next city over.

Bea and her friend Maggie had just graduated from their tiny local high school, which was housed in an old wooden sawmill that had been converted into a school. Bea had no idea what to do with her life, nor did she have any idea what was in store for her.

Bea had big ideas of maybe moving to the city somewhere, but the truth was that she loved the little town she lived in. She always joked with Maggie that if she stayed in their little town for too long, she would grow old and die a lonely old maid. Bea was a romantic and always had these wild dreams of some kind of prince or knight in shining armor, that would ride into town, swoop her off her feet, and she would spend her life living in some fantastical castle on a mountain. I wouldn't be a bit surprised if Bea had also imagined fairies and leprechauns surrounding her castle and bringing her fresh fruits and berries every day. Bea had a great imagination, and she used it to imagine great things.

However, everyone's imaginations, dreams, and plans were on hold. There was a war on. A big war. Most of the eligible young men were being shipped off to Europe and elsewhere to fight. With the young men gone, any hopes of dating, or princes, or knights in shining armor, were on hold. Adult women were left with the challenge of filling all the full-time jobs left vacant by the men who were in the war. There wasn't much of a chance for women to accept the courting of men, or keep a nice home. Women were the workforce that kept the town and the country as a whole running. All of the traditional family dreams had to be placed on hold.

However, all of the discouraging gloom and doom did not keep Bea from finding a way to begin romantic adventures. One day there was some sort of delivery man who was posting notices about the military looking for women to be pen pals to the troops. As soon as the man posted the notice at the entrance of the bakery, Bea was the first one to run over there and read it.

Bea yelled over to Maggie to come read the notice. Bea was already excited. Bea said to Maggie, "Look, this is how I am going to find my man, and he's even going to have the uniform of a knight." Maggie laughed at her and said those pen pal things were only for desperate young girls who wanted to swoon over men, and pretend someday the men would love them back. Bea was not discouraged by Maggie's wet towel over her vision of a young man in uniform. Bea simply exclaimed, "I'm doing it!" Maggie just laughed and said, "Well then I'll be right here waiting for your wedding invitation."

Bea followed through with her plan to sign up for the pen pal program. She wrote her first letter, even though she had no idea who she was writing to. One of her lines in that first letter was, "I don't even know you, but I want all your dreams to come true someday."

It took a long time, but one day Bea received a reply. A soldier named George had been given Bea's letter, and had been assigned as her pen pal. George wrote to Bea thanking her for her very nice letter. One of George's first lines was "I don't have the pleasure of knowing you in person, but any woman who would wish for my dreams to come true, is a woman worth having all of her own dreams come true." It was kind of corny, but still sweet. Bea was happy with it anyway. George went on to say he was stationed in an area of Europe that was seeing heavy action and he never knew what would happen the next day. He briefly described his background as having grown up in a rural town, but no longer had any family that he stayed in touch with. His mother had passed away of an illness, and after a childhood full of clashing with his father, he was disowned by his father on his 18th birthday. He enlisted in the military because his life back home seemed to have no meaning, and thought maybe he could make a difference in the world by enlisting in the military.

George seemed especially interested in where Bea lived and what her life was like. These were the exact subjects that Bea was trying to avoid because she felt her little life in her little town would be so boring to George that he might fall asleep and have no further interest in corresponding. However, the opposite was true, because George found a small-town life very appealing.

George was a young man full of dreams. He was a very intelligent and motivated 18-year-old who wanted to conquer the world, but do it in a meaningful family atmosphere. George's own negative family experiences left him wanting to build his own family even more. Before the war, George had dreams of finding the love of his life, providing a loving home for his children, and having his own business that would build loving homes for everyone else. George wanted to literally build homes. He had dreams of becoming a builder and owning his own contracting company.

Much of this resonated with Bea. Bea came from a family that owned their own business, loved making a difference for local families, and Bea had also envisioned herself having a family with children playing in the grass and enjoying the wonderful wholesome upbringing that she had benefited from.

George's intelligence, motivation, and his unfortunate but interesting current travels were very intriguing to Bea. Bea once told Maggie that corresponding with George made her feel like a hometown girl living a sophisticated life full of travel, culture, philosophy, business, and politics, because George was so well versed and interested in many subjects. Bea felt she could just sit and stare at George for hours and listen to him speak if she only had the chance. Bea especially felt this after she finally saw a photo of George and realized how handsome he was. It was not expected that pen pals would exchange photos, but in George and Bea's case, it turned out there was a definite physical attraction between them after they did.

As time went on and the letters starting stacking up, the pen pal arrangement turned into a full-fledged long-distance romance. George was very smitten with Bea and was saying all the right things to her. Bea was very captivated by George and became very devoted to him. Her devotion to George got to the level of her starting to write George every day. George could not respond as often, but he always acknowledged every letter within his summary and regular correspondence when he was able to send one out.

George acknowledged to Bea that her letters kept him going during very dark times, and that she made him feel like he was "home." Bea took this as her cue to provide further comfort to George as much as she could. Bea started including things like blades of grass from the park inside her letters to George. So, George would get his letter overseas and be able to actually hold and feel a piece of "home," which in this case was grass from Bea's local park.

For Bea's Christmas package to George, she filled the little box with evergreen sprigs and a pine cone she got from the park. The remaining space was filled with cookies and treats from her family's shop. George enjoyed the package immensely and said it made him feel as if he was really there.

Over the many months to come, Bea continued with her daily letters, but also sent packages quite often. Inside the packages, Bea continued to send blades of grass and pine cones, along with various cookies and treats for George and some of his military buddies.

It was certainly inevitable that the two wanted to be together, were emotionally already together, and had pretty much already decided to share their lives together. Bea started to convince George to move to her town when he was finally released from the military. George of course wanted this, but George had no money, and thus no way to have a place to live for himself, let alone for the two of them together.

George gently let Bea know that he did not come from money and would have to find a way to start over after the military, and then perhaps after he had some money saved, he could join Bea in her town. Bea was not having any of this talk. Bea reacted by impulsively inviting George to come stay with her at her family's home until he could get settled. Bea made it sound like her family had plenty of room, and of course mentioned that they owned their own store that sold bakery items and treats, including those she had been sending him.

Thinking that Bea MOST SURELY had secured approval of this idea from her family, he agreed that it was a wonderful idea, and he agreed to "move" directly to her town once he was released from duty.

Of course, there was one small problem. Bea had NOT secured approval from her family, nor did she even mention any of this to her parents. However, that was only a minor detail to Bea, who never let anything stop her from getting what she wanted. Besides, her parents already knew about her budding romance with this soldier through the pen pal program. Her parents would not be totally shocked about Bea wanting to continue the relationship.

Finally, Bea had the very tense and awkward conversation with her parents, informing them that she had already kind of invited George to stay with them. She tempered and exaggerated her presentation by telling her parents that George had no place to go back to, that we should all support our troops when they come back home, and that George would only stay for a short time until he could get settled.

Based upon this presentation, Bea's parents reluctantly agreed to allow George to stay with them temporarily, under the condition he would of course have to stay in the guest room. Bea was thoroughly excited, and then did indeed confirm to George that her parents were totally approving of the idea, and that they were very excited to have him staying with the family. Yep, Bea always knew how to accentuate and exaggerate a point in her favor.

Eventually, the day finally came when George was given notice that he was coming home for good. Both of them were beyond excited to finally be with each other in person, and George said the very first thing he wanted to do after stepping off the bus, was to stroll with his first and only love to the park that they so often talked about. Bea replied with, "It's a date!"

Well, that day finally arrived. George was due to arrive into town on the bus at noon. Bea was nervous, but much more excited than nervous. She had made herself all beautiful and gussied up in the most cheerful outfit she could put together. It was a cloudy day threatening rain, but Bea wanted to dress like it was the brightest most sunny day of the year.

Maggie was helping her get ready, and Bea was telling Maggie that after so long in the military where everything is one drab color, she figured George would appreciate some color and cheer. As with most excited young girls, it took hours for her to feel she was properly prepared to receive George at the bus station.

Bea was not going to be the only one greeting George at the bus station though. Maggie insisted, because she claimed she had participated through all of the drama the entire term of this long-distance relationship, and thus deserved to see the man in person without having to wait another minute.

But that was not the worst of it. Bea's parents also insisted on going (*ouch*). Bea's parents were NOT about to let their daughter meet some strange man at a bus station, especially since such man was going to be staying in THEIR home. There was no arguing about this, although Bea gave it her best effort. A compromise was reached, and Bea's parents promised to not ask George any questions.

So, Bea and her entire entourage arrived at the bus station and waited for George's arrival. Finally, the big bus arrived. Bea stood up close to the bus while her entourage at least stayed a safe distance in the back. It felt like a ton of people got off that bus, but no George yet. He must have been sitting in the back, because when everyone had gotten off, the last man to exit the bus was a very tall and dashing young man.

Bea knew it was George. And George knew it was Bea. George looked way more handsome in person, and he looked even better in that military uniform. Bea felt she had hit the jackpot. George gave Bea a little wave and a smile, and that was the only invitation Bea needed to rush him and nearly tackle him. She ran into his arms and they embraced while Bea's parents looked on in surprise as their daughter acted as if she had known this stranger for years.

Maggie and Bea's parents walked up to join the excitement. George looked over to notice Bea had an unexpected entourage. But instead of being freaked out, he seemed to take it in stride, showing not a single flinch or hesitation. He introduced himself to Bea's father first, as if he knew where the power center of the entourage was located. Bea's father seemed to really like this, and thus seemed to develop an immediate liking for George.

Next, George introduced himself to Bea's mother in a most elegant way that almost made her blush. Finally, George looked at Maggie, who was pretty much panting like an excited dog, and he said, "And you must be Maggie!" Maggie seemed thrilled that he already knew her and acknowledged her existence.

Bea's mother then started asking George a thousand questions. Things like,

"How was your trip?"

"How long was your trip?"

"When was the last time you ate?"

"Are you hungry?"

"Do you need a good rest?"

The questions kept coming in rapid-fire never seeming to end, with George having no chance to answer them even if he tried. Bea piped up and said,

"MOM YOU PROMISED!" Bea's mom then said,

"Oh yes, sorry dear, I will stop talking now."

This elicited a laugh from George, as if George had figured out what the arrangement must have been between them.

However, George did sort of answer the questions with one statement. He said,

"With all due respect, what I would love to do most right now is accompany Bea for a nice walk to this park that is supposed to be around here somewhere."

Bea looked at her father and said,

"Oh can we dad, is that okay?" Her father looked at George, and then Bea, and said,

"Yes, sure that would be fine."

Bea's mother then offered to George that they would take his duffle bag for him, and it would be waiting for him back at the house. George was delighted and thanked her profusely.

Off they went. Only Bea and George that is. Fortunately, Maggie did not need it explained to her that she was not invited on this particular leg of the adventure. George took Bea's arm, and then hoped for Bea to lead the way since George had no idea where he was going. Bea and George talked as if they had always known each other. It was incredibly natural that some might have found it disconcerting (in a good way). They had only met each other in person ten minutes ago, and they acted as if they were a long-engaged couple.

Before they knew it, they had arrived at the park. George took a very long look around as if to give it a very hard military inspection. Bea asked him if something was wrong. George replied that nothing was wrong. He just said how it was almost exactly as he had imagined, and that he couldn't believe he was actually there in real life.

Bea grabbed George's hand and started showing him around the park. There was not much to see specifically, but to everyone who spent a lot of time at the park, there were indeed certain things to show. There were the different types of trees, for example. Mostly there were oak and maple trees, but the park did have those few huge pine trees that dropped the now famous and important pine cones. Bea felt it was important to point those out to George.

George seemed to love and appreciate the full "tour," and they started walking to this nice open grassy part not far from the woodline, and George stopped and asked if they could just sit on the grass for a bit. So, that is what they did. They sat on the grass in this lovely spot that seemed to be made just for them. George even said to Bea, "Let's call this our special spot." Bea agreed while smiling and giggling.

After they had enjoyed their new special spot for a while, those dark clouds decided to open up. It started to rain. George seemed concerned that Bea would be out in the rain, but to his surprise, Bea was LOVING IT. Bea took George's hand and said,

"Even in the rain I am happy with you."

George said, "Well in that case, how much happier would you be if we danced in the rain?"

Bea exclaimed, "VERY HAPPY!"

And so they danced in the rain. They danced as if it was not raining at all. They acted as if they were the only two people on Earth. They had totally gotten lost within each other's eyes. They frolicked in the rain, dancing and laughing, as if they were both children. They danced until the rain stopped, and then they stopped for just a moment. They looked into each other's soul, and their lips met. It was their first kiss. And then there was a second kiss, but the second kiss was much more substantial.

They were in love before they had met in person, but now they were in love more than could be adequately described. At this point I could say, "and the rest is history," but nope. There is too much more to tell.

They walked back to Bea's parent's house and arrived inside soaking wet. Bea's mother immediately showed George to the guest room where he would be staying, and supplied him with fresh towels and showed him the bathroom, and made him feel at home, and well equipped enough to settle in.

This arrangement with George staying in the guest room went on for about a month. Bea's parents were wondering where this was all heading, and what to do about the situation. Bea's parents managed a private moment with Bea at the bakery store and asked her how long George would be staying. Bea of course answered that George needed to stay longer. This is when Bea's mother spoke up and said that if she and George were going to continue living under one roof, they would need to get married so that it would be all proper.

I am not sure if Bea's mother intended for this to scare off Bea or scare off George, but it had the opposite effect. It caused George and Bea to decide that they would marry. The proposal was very private and personal to them, but we know for sure it happened in the park while standing at their exact "special place," as they had designated it previously.

After their very private proposal moment in the park, they both gleefully marched back home to Bea's parent's house. Bea and George informed Bea's parents of the news, and her parents seemed quite approving, despite the short time they had been together as a couple. Within fifteen minutes, Bea's mother was already clucking about all kinds of plans for the wedding. I guess that is the moment when you know you have mom's approval.

Planning for Bea and George's wedding began in earnest. There was an obvious motivation to rush it, since them staying together under the same roof would not be fully embraced by Bea's parents until they were married.

George did not have any money, nor did Bea. Bea's father graciously offered to provide for a proper wedding, but George felt uncomfortable imposing on them for something so gratuitous, and the truth of the matter was that George and Bea actually WANTED a small and simple wedding. While Bea always had stars in her eyes, deep in her heart she was a very private small-town girl who focused on the most precious things in life, such as simply being with the one you love. For Bea, a meaningful romantic picnic at the park was more appealing than fancy ceremonies, expensive jewelry, or other such things that most young ladies yearned for.

It was agreed that it would be a very simple and small wedding that would be held in the park. George and Bea were very sentimental, and it was important to them that the ceremony itself be held right at the "special spot." Bea only wanted flowers surrounding the area and that was all. Bea loved flowers, and that would be her one item of indulgence. Bea's parents enthusiastically agreed to make that happen.

They set a date which was only a few weeks out, and everyone did their part to organize the small affair. There were no invitations to send out since hardly anyone would be there, and that simplified things. George had nobody to attend for him as his Best Man. He smartly asked Bea's father to stand in as his Best Man, after he was done walking Bea down the grassy aisle. The only others in attendance would be Bea's mother obviously, and Maggie would be the Matron of Honor. "Always the bridesmaid and never the bride," Maggie exclaimed in agony, as everyone chuckled. Officiating the ceremony would be one of the town officials, who was authorized to do so.

The magical day for the low-key and unassuming wedding ceremony had arrived, and the tiny wedding party were all in place at the exact special spot, in that very special park that meant so much to George and Bea. The ceremony was performed, and the only thing of note was the addition of one additional vow said by both George and Bea. That vow, or more like statement, was, "I promise to make your dreams come true."

Pretty much immediately after the wedding, George and Bea wanted to move in together into their own private place. They had no money and George had no job, but as their wedding present Bea's parents offered to pay the first three months rent on this very tiny studio apartment not far from the bakery store. George and Bea were beyond excited, and George was eternally grateful for the nice gesture and the much-needed help.

The newlywed couple had no money, but they had each other. They were truly happier in their tiny little studio apartment than your average married couple was in their large family home. Due to the lack of funds and the fact that the gift from Bea's parents was in the form of helping with the apartment, there were no addition source of funds for a honeymoon of any kind.

George felt very guilty for not being able to give Bea a big expensive fabulous diamond ring, or any kind of wedding gift at all, or even a honeymoon. George promised that someday he would make it all up to her. Bea accepted his promise, not caring about the material things, but was just grateful to be with her very handsome man of her dreams.

George and Bea subsisted by working part time in the bakery store for her parents, while George also accepted part time work doing construction. George was just doing basic laborer tasks, such as moving building supplies around, cleaning equipment, and helping the contractors. It always resulted in a small paycheck, but he was learning a lot about the contracting business doing it. With both of them working together, cobbling together small paychecks, they were able to barely get by, and were able to pay their rent after the first three months of free rent were up.

However, Christmas was right around the corner, and there were no extra funds for either of them to get each other anything for Christmas. But frankly, they didn't really care. They cut down a tiny little evergreen for a Christmas tree, decorated it with handmade ornaments, and they made the best of it.

Bea had a great idea to promote her parent's Christmas treats that they sold at the store, and talked to her father about her idea. She wanted to give away a certain number of Christmas trays to a number of the neighbors up and down the streets in the immediate neighborhood. Her father approved of the idea, and Bea spent a lot of time putting together these Christmas gift platters and delivering them unannounced by surprise to many of the neighbors.

It was a fantastic idea that was loved and embraced by the neighbors receiving such a nice gesture and blessing. It resulted in something very unexpected. Before long, some neighbors were buying platters from the store, or making their own, and they were gifting them to other neighbors, who then started doing the same to THEIR neighbors, and so on it went. Before long, half the town was gifting each other Christmas gift trays.

It was a great business for the bakery store, since they made Christmas treats during the season, but plenty of neighbors also made their own at home, and that was embraced as well. This thing of exchanging Christmas gift trays between neighbors continued every year thereafter, and still lives on today. At least in this town, they have Bea to thank for that.

However, as Christmas Day approached, both George and Bea grew anxious about what they could give each other as Christmas gifts. Neither one was expecting anything, but each still wanted to give something anyways.

Bea finally thought of a wonderful idea.

Remember all those pine cones Bea had sent to George overseas?

Well, George kept *all* of those pine cones, and when he got sent back home, he brought all of them back with him.

It was Bea's idea to take all of those pine cones that meant so much to both of them, and she would use glue and construct a cute little house out of them. So, yes, she made a little house model made of pine cones. To her it represented them building a nice home someday from the love they shared together.

As for George, he thankfully also came up with a great idea of his own. George had been busy constructing something for Bea while she was busy working or doing other things.

On Christmas day, their first Christmas living together, Bea was the first to present her gift to George. At first sight of the jumble of pine cones glued together, George was not sure what it was supposed to be, and they both looked at each other and laughed. But then Bea started to explain, and told him that those were HIS pine cones, and George grew this incredible look of glee on his face. He had never imagined such a clever idea in his life. He absolutely loved his little pine cone house and was obviously very touched.

Then George said to Bea, "You don't actually think I would not have something for you on Christmas, do you?" Bea kind of shrugged because she didn't see anything laying around the apartment for her, nor did she have her hopes up for anything. George told her to get her coat on and that they were going for a walk.

George led Bea to the park. As they walked across the park to their special spot, Bea could see there was something new there. Walking up to it, Bea could see sitting there was a very primitive bench, built of logs and sticks with nails. Bea looked confused, and George said to her, "What, you don't like the bench I built for you?" Bea started laughing and was in shock. George started laughing also. George said, "I know it's not much, but it's the best I could do with the branches and things I found here in the park; Merry Christmas my love."

George motioned for Bea to take a seat. At first, Bea looked afraid to even sit on it, as it might collapse under the weight, but she gave it a go. She sat down and it didn't break. George then applauded her for being such a good sport and sitting on it. George then said, "I promise that I will build you a better one." Bea replied by saying, "Okay but I love this one." They both knew it was a polite little lie she was telling, but it was sweet. That first Christmas was remembered by them as their most special.

George and Bea continued along, enjoying their life together. Soon they would have major news to share with everyone. Bea was expecting a child! Their little circle of family and friends rejoiced. This little child would be born into one of the most loving families ever. I think George and Bea's excitement was only exceeded by Bea's mother's and father's, who were overjoyed at the prospect. It gave everyone in the family a new center of focus, and a motivation to build their family and environment into the best it could be.

George, however, also felt a huge weight on his shoulders. He immediately realized that his little part-time jobs doing menial low-paying labor, were not going to work long-term with a new child coming. Thus, George decided to start his own contracting business.

George started going after very small jobs, such as doing interior repairs to houses, and some minor renovation work, and so forth. No job was too small for George. He called his business "George's Contracting." He pretty much relied on people who knew Bea's family, who wanted to help them out by giving jobs to George instead of one of the larger contracting companies.

George was not the most experienced, but he operated with complete integrity, and would go back to jobs that weren't right and would make them right. He guaranteed his work, and always delivered a personal touch. The reputation of his genuine service and work ethic quickly spread, and he soon had more work than he could handle.

George hired some other workers to help him, and his little business grew. It got to such a point that George decided he would try to buy a house lot, build a house, and sell it. There was much more money in that, than just doing small jobs for various people.

George looked around and found a nice deal on two house lots located not far from where they lived. Although he had a nice income, he didn't have any extra cash laying around. He saw an advertisement from some out-of-state bank that was trying to increase their loan business, and was offering easy access to funds to new borrowers. George inquired with that bank, and it was explained that the bank was offering "lines of credit." This meant that it was not a real estate loan, and did not require current real estate ownership to be approved for the loan. Instead, it was basically a "credit card loan," where George could draw funds from the line of credit at any time for any purpose, up to the limit of the loan. In return, George only needed to make the interest payments on time, and could repay the loan at any time he was able.

The bank saw that George was doing well with his little contracting business, and agreed to approve his line of credit. George promptly used his line of credit to buy the two house lots, and he would use the remainder to pay for materials needed to build the first house. He would have to provide the labor without pay, and he would have no more line of credit remaining to use. It was risky, but George felt it was the only way to take the next step in growing his business.

George and Bea were optimistic, and George continued to work at his business and his new real estate deal, while Bea was in charge of taking care of her pregnancy and the baby on the way. It was a busy time for them both, but a very happy time full of optimism for the future. They were finally going to have the family they had always wanted!

Despite being super busy with his business, George made time for one very important task. He had a pregnant wife, with a baby on the way, and he had made a promise that he wanted to keep. George really wanted to build that new park bench that he had promised Bea. The bench that was sitting at the park presently, was just made of sticks and scraps, and was just meant as a funny gesture and heart-felt Christmas gift. Surely, that stick bench was not worthy or safe for a pregnant wife, let alone a wife with a baby. George decided to go ahead and build a new park bench made of quality materials that would be strong, safe, and would last a very long time.

He built the bench in his shop, and took his time so that it would be exactly the way he wanted it. He used high quality wood strapping and assembled it all so that it would remain solid far into the future. He coated the wood so that it would not rot. It was a very nice and new shiny work of art when he was finished.

When he knew Bea wouldn't be at the park or see any activity over there, he had his new bench installed in the exact location of the present bench. The present bench was only sticks and logs anyways, but it had become sentimental, so he decided to keep one piece of wood (branch) from it, so that he and Bea would have a fond memory they could hold onto and look back on whenever they wanted.

Once the new bench was installed, he brought Bea over to the park to surprise her with it. He told her that he had a baby gift for her. For the life of her she could not figure out what kind of "baby gift" would be sitting in a park, rather than in their apartment. Once she arrived and started walking over to their special spot where the previous log and stick bench had been, she realized what it was.

She could see that brand new shiny bench gleaming in the sun. She started to cry. She saw how beautiful it was and what an amazing job George had done building it. She had no hesitation about sitting down on this bench and trying it out. George told Bea that he built this bench to last, and that it should last longer than him. George sat down with her, and they both enjoyed the view from the comfort of their new bench. That bench would become their second home for many years to come.

Bea's pregnancy advanced, and everything seemed to be fine and on track for an on-time delivery. George and Bea spent a lot of time gathering all of the baby supplies they would need. Bea's parents along with Maggie and her father, contributed generously to the collection of baby supplies, equipment, and items needed. It was going to be cramped in their tiny little place, but they made room in the corner for a bassinet, and everything would work out fine for the time being.

Finally, the day arrived when Bea went into labor. Bea's parents took George and Bea to the hospital, and Bea was admitted to a delivery room. Bea's parents waited in the waiting area, and George waited with Bea in the delivery room.

Once contractions were regular and the baby was coming, George was asked if he could wait outside in the waiting area where he might be more comfortable. George kissed Bea on the cheek, told her she would do great, and he left the room to meet up with Bea's parents.

The delivery took what seemed like an eternity. But it didn't just *seem* that way. It indeed was taking way longer than usual. After many hours, the doctor came into the waiting room and asked to speak with George alone. Slightly concerned, George went with the doctor to another empty room.

The doctor had some very bad news. The doctor explained that there were some complications with the baby that they had not anticipated. There had been something wrong with the pregnancy, the way the baby was positioned, and the way the cord was wrapped around the baby's neck somehow. The doctor explained that if there had been only ONE problem, he likely could have managed the situation, but there were separate problems with both Bea and the baby.

The doctor looked at George and said, "I'm sorry but I couldn't save your baby." George nearly fell to the ground, but then desperately asked, "But is Bea okay?" The doctor assured him that Bea was stable and resting comfortably.

However, the doctor had one more piece of news to deliver. The doctor explained that due to the complications and issues with Bea, along with this failed pregnancy and delivery, Bea would not be able to have any children in the future. George asked the doctor if Bea knew this, and the doctor said that he had already told Bea everything that he just said to him. George knew Bea must be devastated, and asked if he could see her. The doctor said "Of course." George went into the recovery room where Bea was lying there with a vacant defeated look on her face. George went over to Bea and took her hand. Bea looked at George and said,

"I'm sorry I failed you."

George said to Bea, "You did not fail me; you have never failed me."

Bea then said, "I can never have..," and George interrupted her before she could finish.

He said, "I know." Bea just stared up at the ceiling. George sat silently, processing everything that had happened, and thinking about what all this meant for them and their lives.

Bea then said, "I can't make your dreams come true."

George looked at Bea right in the eyes, touched her cheek gently with his finger, and said,

"You are the love of my life, and just being with you makes my dreams come true every day." He continued, "Nothing that happened today has changed that whatsoever."

He then smiled at her reassuringly. Tears started slowly streaming from her eyes, and she said to him,

"I don't deserve a husband as good as you, but I am grateful every day I have you anyways."

George and Bea then embraced as well as they could considering she was in a hospital bed. After that, George did his best to talk about other things and get her mind off of the events of the day.

George eventually went back out to the waiting area to speak with Bea's parents. He could see by their glum appearance that they already knew. He told them that Bea would stay the night at the hospital, that he would sleep in the chair next to her, and that they would manage a way home tomorrow. However, Bea's parents told George there was no way they were leaving their daughter at this time, and that they would get a hotel room and drive them all back home tomorrow. And that is what happened. They all were able to go back home the next day.

When Bea was able to walk more easily and get around, she and George had one very sad piece of business to take care of. Their baby had been still-born, and they had requested the remains to be cremated so they could at least have those. The package with the ashes arrived by special courier, and it was time to place the ashes in an appropriate final resting place.

George and Bea decided they would bury the baby's ashes in a remote wooded corner of the park. It would be a place that was out of the way, very discrete, but a beautiful place, and a place they could go to anytime and visit the resting place of their little baby.

George had managed to find a stone post of granite that nobody was using or needed. They decided to bury the ashes and place the granite stone post as a marker. They did not want to engrave anything on the marker though. They wanted to keep it very private and discrete, so that only they would know what it was.

So, on a very early morning while dawn was just barely breaking, they interned the ashes, and placed the stone marker. They cried, they said a prayer, and they held each other in embrace while looking at the site. They were both very broken inside, but still very devoted to each other. Even a tragedy this horrible would not break their impenetrable bond.

As if the loss of their baby was not enough, along with the news that Bea could never have a child in the future, the bad news did not stop coming. One day George received a notice from the bank with which he had his line of credit. The notice said that the bank was canceling his line of credit, and per the loan agreement, the loan was due in full within thirty days.

George was confused and in shock. How could the bank do that on a whim for no reason? George had not missed a single interest payment, and things in general were still going very well for George's business. He contacted the bank and talked to them about it. He explained to the bank that he had spent the entire line of credit to buy two house lots and building materials to start building a house, which he would then be able to sell at a nice profit. He explained to the bank that he did not have any money to pay off the loan, nor could he sell off the building lots fast enough to pay off the loan.

The bank's reply was that they were sorry to hear this, but their board of directors had decided to change their policies regarding the line of credits, and to cancel all of the line of credits they had given. The banker explained that George was not the only one affected by this new policy, and he was very sorry for the inconvenience. George replied,

"You are sorry for the INCONVENIENCE? Don't you realize this will bankrupt me?" Without hesitation, the banker just said,

Again, I am sorry, but we must insist on holding you to the terms of the contract, and those terms state that we may cancel a line of credit at any time, and demand immediate payment in thirty days."

There seemed nothing George could do. When the thirty days was up, George was unable to pay off the line of credit. The bank filed papers to sue him and seize all of his property to secure payment of the loan. George lost his house lots, the building materials, plus he still owed a balance, which caused him to lose all of his equipment, which then left no money to pay his workers, and thus he couldn't even finish the customer jobs that were in progress. George was essentially bankrupt and out of business just like that. It was over. He was ruined. He had lost his growing business, his hopes, his dreams, and his income. He was broken with nowhere to turn, and no way to recover.

George and Bea were devastated, and plunged into a very dark time. Bea felt she had failed as a wife and a mother by losing their child, in addition to not being able to ever provide a family to George in the future. George felt he had failed as a husband and provider from his business crashing and burning, leaving him with no apparent hope of ever reaching success. The two had lost everything, and neither felt there was any chance of happiness, or anything resembling what they had both dreamt of and promised each other.

Their entire relationship had begun on the premise that they wanted to make each other's dreams come true. Here they were with both of them having all of their dreams crushed. For most other couples, this likely would have also doomed their relationship and marriage. However, there was some magic between George and Bea that would not be snuffed out.

One day, George suggested to Bea that they take a walk together to the park. There was not much else to do, so why not? George grasped Bea's hand as they walked down the street to the park. When they arrived at the park, it was as if the cloudy sky parted ways to let the sun shine through. There was literally a ray of sunlight hitting upon the grass on one particular spot at the park right in front of their bench. George pulled Bea, almost running, over to that spot where the sun was hitting the grass next to the bench.

George bent over and picked some blades of grass. He showed them to Bea in his hand and said, "These blades of grass you used to send me in your letters represented my dreams of a home, love, and family." He continued, "As long as this grass and you are here with me, my dreams are still alive." Bea tearing up and gently crying. She had been so broken, but George was showing her that maybe dreams don't die so easily, and maybe she had not destroyed all of George's dreams.

For her part, Bea grabbed the blades of grass from George's hand and said, "As long as new blades of grass can grow in this park we so love, I am certain we can also grow." She continued, "As old grass dies, new grass grows to take its place." She said with tears in her eyes while gazing directly into George's eyes, "I believe in you even more now than I did at any time before." She continued, "I know you can build and grow anything you set your mind on doing."

George, who had been feeling like a total failure, got tears in his eyes, and looking at Bea, said,

"I pledge to you Bea, that whenever something fails to grow and survive, I will simply re-grow and rebuild, such that your dreams never die."

Bea replied, "As long as we are together and working together to make things grow, my dreams will never die."

The two embraced each other tightly while standing in that beautiful ray of sunlight, and tears streaming down both their faces. Love had survived.

George led Bea over to their bench and they sat down. George, holding Bea's hand said, "I proclaim this bench to be the bench of love and dreams." He continued on, "Whatever sadness might exist on this bench from time to time, let happiness and love always prevail upon this bench." He said, "Love is never letting someone's dreams die." And with that pledge, their dreams had survived also.

That is not all that happened that day. While walking back home from the park, they were passing Bea's family bakery, when the front door flung open, and out flew Maggie running right toward them. Maggie seemed very excited, almost desperately so. Maggie explained that she had a miracle of good news for them, and specifically George. Bea's parents then walked out of the store to wave for George and Bea to come inside.

George, Bea, and Maggie quickly scurried into the store. Bea's parents in a very serious and genuine way, looked directly at George and said to him, "We have been talking here, and we have been looking for a way to invest some money that we have been saving from our years of built-up savings earned from this store." They continued on, "We have decided the best investment we could ever make would be to invest with you George, in having you start another contracting business, if that is what you choose to do."

George looked at them stunned with his mouth half open. Bea was equally shocked, except with a hint of pride and gratitude along with her shock. George looked like he didn't know what to say. Then Maggie piped up and said, "That's not all though." Maggie continued, "I talked to my father, and he has pledged to sign on any loan you might need from his local bank, to start over again."

Now George and Bea were both totally stunned and frozen with shock. They looked at each other and started embracing again. George tried to hide his tears, but Bea made no such effort. At the sight of it all, Bea's parents and Maggie joined in with the tears of joy.

Bea only broke the embrace to quietly show George something. Bea opened her hand to show George that she was holding the blades of grass from the park in her hand. Bea whispered to George, "Our dreams will never die, and neither will our love."

Well, it wasn't very easy, but George was able to get restarted again. He decided to call his new business "Carlisle Construction Company," since his full name was George Carlisle. He had to start small, but it was not long before Carlisle Construction Company was very busy doing home renovations, building barns, garages, and acting as subcontractors on some bigger commercial building projects outside of town.

George was getting a lot of experience with all different types of construction, and was building a reputation for integrity and quality once again. People loved doing business with his company, and he was no longer at the mercy of the out-of-state banks, thus not as vulnerable to failure as before.

His business turned out to be a self-fulfilling prophecy of success. People trusted him to do their building projects, workers loved working for him, and that just led to more business, which led to more workers, which led to buying more equipment, which led to more jobs, which led to more workers, and so forth. It just sort of grew on its own after a while, mostly based upon George's initial premise of integrity.

George gradually became one of the largest employers in the area. He was the building contractor of choice for not only that area, but also in neighboring cities and states. George's company and the town seemed to be growing symbiotically. George's company was buying up all the empty house lots on many of the local streets, and then building nice quality homes on those lots.

All of the local people preferred to buy Carlisle homes because they knew who George was, most knew him personally, and they knew George would stand behind his work. And George DID stand behind his work. He was one of the first builders to offer comprehensive home warranties. He was also one of the first builders to offer easy financing and home insurance options through his own finance company which worked directly with commercial banks, and his insurance company subsidiary.

It was not long before George also had appliance stores, building materials stores, flooring and window treatment stores, furniture stores, a roofing company, a cement factory, and various other ventures. George's empire stretched across three states.

The large bank which had destroyed George the first time around, along with other banks who had shunned him, were now begging to do business with George. Since George controlled much of the housing sales in a huge area, that meant George also had influence over which banks home buyers might consider in financing their homes. Unfortunately for the large out-of-state banks, George had a long memory. He preferred to develop relationships with the small local banks, and was able to arrange easier financing for his home buyers through his arrangements with the local banks who actually WANTED the business, and also had a stake in seeing the local neighborhoods and neighbors succeed and thrive.

Thrive is exactly what the town did. The sparsely developed streets now had rows of nice, new, but affordable homes lining all the streets. People were moving in from other areas to work for the Carlisle family of companies, as well as all of the other small businesses that were popping up in the area.

George and Bea Carlisle became the most respected people in town, as well as the surrounding areas. It was not just because they were extremely successful and wealthy though. It was because they ran their businesses with integrity, and were very generous to those needing help. They donated money publicly, but also privately. They made some high-profile donations, such as to establish their very own fire department. But they would also give privately, especially to families with children who were struggling.

Sometimes it was just small things like back-to-school shopping money, food for the holidays, or even such things as helping with mortgage relief for families, if someone couldn't work due to illness or some other unfortunate circumstance. How this worked was that George would simply make a phone call and negotiate directly with the bank to allow a temporary halt in payments. The back payments would then be factored back into the loan over time, or on the back-end of the loan. The bank would agree to do this because if they did not, George could simply start directing lending business away from them.

George and Bea basically became everyone's family, parents, and grandparents. While George and Bea could not have children of their own, that was replaced by being parents to the entire town. The entire town looked up to them, and the Carlisles took care of everyone in town as if they were their own kin. George and Bea's dream of having a family had come true in a very unexpected way.

There was a gradual movement in town of some people calling the Carlisles "Momma B" and "Daddy G." George and Bea looked after everyone as if they were their own child. If someone needed help, there was a good chance that Bea and George would end up helping them in some direct or indirect way if they could. Only once in the town's history was there a problem, and a need, so big that perhaps even the Carlisles would not be able to solve it.

Despite the town growing and busting at the seams, the high school was still housed in an old wooden building that was formerly the old saw mill. The building was ancient, it was small, and it was in disrepair. The towns people often joked how every street in town was lined with brand new Carlisle homes, but the high school was one of the oldest and most broken-down buildings in the area. That may have been an exaggeration, but there was enough truth to it that it became an uncomfortable reality that something needed to be done.

Most of the town residents were not sure what to do. Everyone was already paying substantial property taxes, including huge tax bills paid by the Carlisle businesses, but it seemed to only be enough to cover all the basic expenses of the town. How could the town possibly afford to build a brand-new high school that met all of the current codes and standards? These standards required a big concrete block building with state of the art electrical, HVAC, fire protection systems, and everything else that was starting to be required by new state regulations.

There was a big town meeting scheduled to discuss the matter. Ironically, the meeting was to be held at the high school in the very building that was at the core of the issue. It was also the only building big enough to accommodate the large crowd expected. This was a very major issue for the town, and some residents were terrified that their taxes would go up to pay for it, and they wouldn't be able to afford to keep their home anymore. It was a valid concern. There were many concerns about the entire situation, and all of them were valid. But the most valid concern of all was that using this building for the high school was no longer sustainable.

Intentionally or not, the school principal at the time made sure the building issues and blemishes were on full display. There were buckets sitting out in places where the roof leaked, for example. I don't think anyone in town disagreed with the current building needing repair, or the need for a new high school though.

It was a packed house. The turnout was huge, and there was barely enough room for all of the residents who were concerned enough to show up. At the start of the meeting, the town officials shared some partial good news with all the residents. They explained that the state had approved the project, and would be paying for a large portion of the new facility. But then they showed how much money they would have to come up with on their own, even after the state paid their share. Very quickly, the discussions began about how much property taxes would have to increase in order to cover the project. The town officials explained how a large bank had agreed to loan the town money for their share of the project, under the condition that there was a specific new tax implemented to cover the payments. Basically, the bank required proof of a new revenue source that would be specifically earmarked to cover the payments to them. Under the circumstances, it sounded quite reasonable, and it seemed the town might have figured out a workable solution.

However, there was a very swift opposing push-back to this solution from homeowners who felt they could not afford a new tax. The discussions started to turn into a huge free-for-all debate, and it was starting to get very passionate and out of control. If this meeting had been held in the cafeteria, there would have been an all-out food fight.

This is when there was an interruption in the meeting. Someone with a very strong authoritative voice yelled from the back of the giant room, "WAIT A MINUTE EVERYONE!"

Everyone looked to the back of the room and saw a tall very distinguished gentleman standing up from his seat. It was none other than George Carlisle. There were some gasps, followed by complete silence. Nobody had noticed him come in, and they naturally assumed he had been too busy to show up. But he had entered through the back, and sat down in the back, after the meeting had already begun.

George said in a civilized calm tone, "May I come up and speak please?"

Well, this was a rhetorical question. When George Carlisle asked to speak, nobody needed to grant him permission. People just let him speak as he wished, whenever he wished, for however long he wished.

With that said, George waited for the town official to grant him permission, which the official obviously did.

George gracefully made his way up to the front where the microphone was located. George had a certain power and dignity about him, and a way of commanding an entire room, and this moment was no exception. Everyone was silent as they watched him walk up front. He was wearing a long business coat, and it was flowing up slightly in the air behind him, as if it was a cape worn by a superhero. Nobody really knew what to expect.

George started to speak. He explained how he understood the problem, and he understood the concerns. He spoke of how this town was his family, and how everyone's child was his child as well. He said there was nothing more important for children than having a great school. He then said that he did not build half the homes in town just for people to struggle staying in them, because of higher taxes that they could not afford.

George then said, "I have a solution."

I swear you could have heard a pin drop from a mile away, that room was so silent in that moment. George explained that he had looked into the matter, and that the state was basically offering to pay for half of the school. He went on to say that he had looked at costs for constructing such a facility that was befitting "all of our children," as he put it. He then suggested that much of the expense could be offset if his construction company built the facility at the base cost of the materials and labor only, with no profit built in. Of course, no construction company would ever agree to do such a project with no profit, except for Carlisle of course.

EVERYONE CHEERED. Nobody even let him finish speak. It was as if everyone had heard all they needed to hear. The crowd interpreted the solution as George offering up his company to build the new high school "at cost," with no mark-ups on materials or labor. Carlisle Construction Company was certainly qualified and capable of such a project. His company had grown to such a large level that they had already built government office buildings in other cities. The fact George would offer Carlisle Construction to do the work at no profit would make a big difference in solving the town's financial problem.

But George wasn't done speaking. He just stood there motionless, waiting for the crowd to be silent again. Once everyone realized he apparently had more to say, they became silent, and George continued his remarks. He explained that even with his company building the facility at cost, there would obviously still be a substantial expense to doing such a large project. Then he made the statement that nobody expected. George said, "My beautiful wife Bea, myself, and Carlisle Construction Company, will be paying for the entire remainder of this project."

There remained an incredible silence in the room as the stunned crowd attempted to process what he had just said. Then, as if everyone in the room figured it out all at the same time, there was a huge roar, which the gymnasium had not experienced since Carlisle High had won a state basketball championship years ago.

The town officials stood in shock, everyone in the room rose up from their chairs to stand, and everyone cheered, with some even having tears in their eyes. Rather than stand up there for as long as people would cheer, George just quietly and calmly walked down the center isle of the room, and walked out of the building.

I can't prove it, but I think that might have been the first very big "mic drop" to ever happen, at least in this next of the woods.

And so it happened. Construction on the new high school began on a large vacant piece of land, which ironically many in town felt the Carlisles might have built their personal estate on. However, the reality was that the Carlisles never intended on building such an estate. Thus, the high school was built on the biggest piece of vacant land that was still within walking distance of the town center and the park.

The project took a good two years, but Carlisle Construction Company spared no expense and cut no corners. The facility turned out much nicer than even the plans had called for. It was a very small town that now had a very modern and nice high school that was beyond the quality of all other schools in the state. Without any request from the Carlisles, and without any discussion in town, the new school was named "Carlisle High School." I think everyone presumed, wanted, and expected it to be named after the Carlisles.

Upon completion of the project, there was a ribbon cutting, and George and Bea were the guests of honor to cut the ribbon. At the ceremony, George simply said, "For all our children," and then he and Bea cut the ribbon. George and Bea Carlisle literally became eternal legends. Their legacy still stands today, although with some renovations and updates having been done throughout the years. The expense of such updates were paid mostly by Carlisle trust grants.

George and Bea enjoyed their success, along with the fame and respect that came with their generosity, but they were never ostentatious about it, and they always remembered where they came from. Remembering how Bea's parents and Maggie's dad had helped George get back on his feet many years ago, George found ways to show his gratitude. George ended up gifting Bea's parents a house. As for Maggie's dad, well, unfortunately he ended up passing away. But George honored Maggie's dad by gifting a house to Maggie. These were probably the two largest private acts of generosity George and Bea did. Most people in town did not realize the Carlisles literally gave away two houses, but the recipients ended up telling close friends of the generous blessing, and thus word discretely spread of these incredible acts of generosity.

Ironically, George and Bea did not shower themselves with much more generosity than they granted to others. They continued to live a very simple life. The inside joke was that the most important thing to George and Bea was their personal time at the park, as well as blades of grass and pine cones. George and Bea were not impressed with big fancy houses or things.

They also did not travel very much. They loved their hometown and rarely left. Just like everyone in town considered them to be their "parents," George and Bea considered everyone in town to be their family. Why would they want to leave their family? They didn't want to, is the answer.

You might think George and Bea would have built themselves a huge mansion to live in. They certainly could have afforded it. But they didn't live in any such place. They lived in quite a modest house. Part of the accepted reasoning for this was because they were modest simple people, but many say the real reason was because George and Bea INSISTED on living very close to the park, and there simply were not any large empty lots available next to the park. There had been the large lot where the new high school had been built, but I think George felt the walk might be too much for them as they aged. Therefore, they had long since passed up the idea of using that land for themselves. Instead they bought up two house lots next to the park, where they built a very nice but relatively modest house. They continued to live in that same house for their entire lives.

The years went by, and George and Bea tried to live more quietly. The attention from them donating the high school was a bit too much for them. They were very private people, and although everyone meant well, it could at times become difficult for them to take a private quiet walk at the park without someone trying to talk to them, or thank them in some way.

Thus, George and Bea became more low-profile. They were getting older, and eventually George retired. He ended up selling most of his businesses. Doing this was helpful in allowing him to be "less relevant" so that they could live in more peace. They remained in their home next to the park, and were often seen going for walks in the park and sitting together on the park bench that George had built for Bea as her "baby gift," even though it was now technically a city park bench, owned by the town.

Eventually George was seen as becoming quite frail. Most people wanted to respect their privacy and not ask too many questions, or gossip much about it. But with that said, it was known by most in town that George was in poor health and not doing well.

While the town gave space to the Carlisles out of respect, you can imagine what this was like for Bea, watching the love of her life start to fade away. Bea and George were both very accepting, and even embracing, of the circle of life. They had lived their entire lives to the fullest, and much of that included "paying it forward." They had no regrets, and were very grateful for all of their blessings, and even more grateful for all of the blessings they had been able to provide for others.

On a personal level, they had shared a love affair that most people only get to read about in books. Their love was the most genuine and natural you could ever hope for. George became increasing weary, and was ready to continue his journey in a different form. Bea was accepting of divine timing and the cycle of life.

On a beautiful sunny day, George, in all his frailty, looked at Bea and nodded to her as if to signal that he felt something happening, and perhaps was sensing that it was his time. Bea laid next to him in bed and they faced each other. Bea said to George, "You made all my dreams come true." George had a tear in one eye, and quietly whispered, "And you made all my dreams come true." Bea then got up from the bed and went to get something from a porcelain container on her makeup table.

She took something out of the container and brought it back to bed with her. She laid back down next to George and showed him what was in his hand. It was a very old dried-up piece of grass. It was blades of grass from that day at the park after they had lost everything except each other.

George looked at it and seemed amused like he wanted to say something, but has having trouble getting any words out, as his breathing seemed to become more labored. Bea put her finger on his lips to signal for him not to speak. Bea then quietly whispered to George, "Our dreams will never die, and neither will our love." She continued, "I'll make sure you are always where the fresh green grass is." George nodded approvingly in agreement. You could tell from his eyes that he had things to say, but no words would come out.

Bea held his hand, and he held hers. To them it felt the same as it did when they held hands that day George arrived off the bus and they strolled in the park. Bea closed her eyes to imagine it was that day again, and she had her soulmate's hand in hers, just like on that day so many years ago. She ended up falling asleep.

When she awoke a short time later, George had moved onto his next journey. George was gone. He had passed silently and peacefully while holding hands with the one woman he ever loved. Bea didn't sob. Bea didn't cry. Bea smiled. She once again put her finger over his lips, as if to say for him to sleep now. Then she caressed George's hand one last time.

A neighbor saw the funeral hearse at the Carlisle's house. The news spread very quickly across town. Without any official announcement from Bea Carlisle, everyone knew what had happened. And without any prompting at all, everyone in town started leaving flowers at the end of Bea's driveway. The hearse had barely left the Carlisle's driveway, and flowers had already started stacking up along the road to their property. Nobody in town had ever seen so many flowers piled up in one place before.

Bea kept her silence and never made any public announcement at all. I guess she figured she didn't need to. She saw everyone knew, and she saw the incredible outpouring of love from the town, and even from people who lived in other towns.

There was no funeral. George left the world the same as he lived in the world. Privately and simply. However, very early on a Sunday morning, someone saw Bea Carlisle spreading George's ashes around the park. Not a single soul invaded her privacy during this act. In fact, nobody even set one foot in any part of the park. She was given the respect and privacy of having the entire park to herself that day. After she seemed to be done spreading George's ashes around the park, she was seen sitting on their bench for hours. While everyone's hearts were broken for her, everyone continued to honor her privacy and there were no intrusions or interruptions for Bea that day.

Shortly after George's ashes were spread in the park, the newspaper ran an article announcing the formation of the "Carlisle Scholarship." Without announcing it herself, Bea had made an enormous donation, and Carlisle High School would now award a scholarship to most any student who needed it, to pay for that student's first year of secondary school. The news was applauded by everyone, but not once did Bea accept or allow any public acknowledgement for it. To this day, each year Carlisle High School still awards quite a few of these scholarships to needy and deserving students.

Years went by, and Bea was able to live mostly unnoticed. She certainly had her routines though, and she would be politely greeted whenever she went to the store, or was seen out and about anywhere. Mostly, she just stayed home and would walk to the park every day, and sit on her bench until she was ready to go back home.

However, with time the bench that was first installed at the time of her pregnancy, had become very old, and all of the repairs and maintenance to keep it going for so many years, could no longer keep up with its decay. Everyone in town knew the bench needed to be replaced, but nobody dared to even suggest such a thing as long as Bea was still around and using the bench.

Bea was a very realistic and sharp old lady though, and she knew the reality of the situation. The story goes that Bea went to the town office one day and asked permission to replace the bench. She was obviously granted permission. Furthermore, the town officials told her that the bench could be replaced by the town maintenance department, and that the new bench would be named after George.

Bea looked at the official and said, "I don't want one single tax dollar to be spent on my account of wanting this bench replaced." She continued, "I will be donating all funds necessary." Nobody ever argued with the Carlisles, so the town official just said, "As you wish ma'am."

A brand-new bench was built and placed in the EXACT same location as the old one. The new bench looked EXACTLY like the old bench, except it had a metal plaque on one of the back strapping boards that said "In loving memory of George Carlisle."

From all accounts, Bea was delighted with the new bench. Still the same, she had requested, and received, one piece of strapping board from the old bench for her to keep. It ended up being one of her most precious treasures, and people reported having seen it leaning up in a corner within what was George's old study.

Bea continued her routine of walking to the park next door and sitting on her bench. However, as time went on, she seemed to go less often, but still often enough to always be seen there by many. Bea would just sit there watching kids, and contemplating various experiences and questions of life.

As Bea sat on her bench contemplating all of her received blessings, and the even greater blessings she was able to give to others, she could not help but be intrigued by a young boy with a funny bowl haircut on a blue and red bicycle talking with his friends. She then thought to herself, "I wonder what amazing things that boy will do and experience in his life." "I hope I might have contributed in some way to making his future better." "If so, then that will have made my life more meaningful, along with my beautiful and wonderful dear George." With that final thought, she just smiled while she sat on her bench watching the children play.

Why might it seem that what should have been the beginning, was the ending?

Or conversely, why does it seem that what logically seemed like it could have been an ending, was the beginning?

The answer is that life itself is not linear.

There is not simply a beginning, middle, and end.

Life is a patchwork of individual stories that combine, and are all somehow interconnected with each other.

More importantly, life is circular rather than linear.

Endings are not the end.

Endings lead to beginnings.

What appears as an ending to us, is simply a transition into a new beginning.

Then round and round we go,

from endings to new beginnings, which lead to endings,

and then another beginning.

We each have a responsibility to keep the circle going.

We accept the lessons and blessings received from those toward their ending who came before us, and we must then create our own lessons and blessings, which we will then turn over to those who shall come after us once we have drawn closer to our so-called ending.

Nobody lives forever, and nobody dies and disappears into oblivion.

We all have our part to play within our divine time as part of the circle. What we think of as an ending for ourselves, is actually a beginning for others who will carry with them all of our lessons, blessings, and passion that we passed onto them.

We honor those who paved the way before us, we do our best to pave our own roads, then we offer as much assistance as possible to those who will pave the road after us. Love for those who came before us, and love for those who will come after us, is what drives the circle to keep turning with greater passion each cycle.

The control we each have, is that we can decide how much of ourselves we invest into the next beginning that shall come after us. The more of ourselves we put into those who will continue the circle after we are gone, the more of ourselves that will continue to live on beyond us through them and others.

Just like the bench…

To further enjoy this series, **"Living A Meaningful Life,"** be sure to check out all of the books in the series below:

Book #1: ***The Bench:*** *Living A Meaningful Life*

Book #2: ***The Farm:*** *Living A Meaningful Life*

Book #3: ***The Lake:*** *Living A Meaningful Life*

Book #4: ***The Favor:*** *Living A Meaningful Life*

Book #5: ***The Promise:*** *Living A Meaningful Life*

Book #6: ***The Sacrifice:*** *Living A Meaningful Life*

Book #7: ***The Challenge:*** *Living A Meaningful Life*

Book #8: ***The Wedding:*** *Living A Meaningful Life*

Book #9: ***The Crew:*** *Living A Meaningful Life*

Book #10: ***The Substitute:*** *Living A Meaningful Life*

Book #11: ***The Graduate:*** *Living A Meaningful Life*

Book #12: ***The Nemesis:*** *Living A Meaningful Life*

Book #13: ***The Proposal:*** *Living A Meaningful Life*

Acknowledgments

Thank you Sarah Delamere Hurding for your editorial assistance, encouragement, and endless support.

Thanks to all of my clients and benefactors who have supported my mission of helping people become greater, stronger, more self-empowered, enlightened, and free of pain.

A special thanks to Ramsey Lewis for his musical inspiration.

ABOUT THE AUTHOR

Brian Hunter is an American Author and Life Coach based in Los Angeles, California. Brian is the author of *The Bench*, *Evolve*, *Heal Me*, *Rising To Greatness*, *The Hunter Equation*, *Aliens*, and *The Walk-In*. His books have sold around the world and have been Best Sellers within their genres. Brian was acknowledged as being intuitive as a child, and then later in life was attributed as having psychic abilities, as chronicled in his dramatic memoir *The Walk-In*. Brian has worked with people from all over the world, including celebrities and captains of industry. Brian was an original cast member of the TV series pilot *Missing Peace*, in which psychics worked with detectives to solve cold cases. He has also worked as an actor and model in Hollywood, and been featured in various movie and TV productions. Brian's current focus is on his writing and life coaching work, helping clients from all walks of life.

www.brianhunterhelps.com

ALSO, BY BRIAN HUNTER

The Farm: Living A Meaningful Life, is Book #2 in the "Living A Meaningful Life" series. *The Farm* is the follow up book to *The Bench*, and continues the journey for the main character, as well as some new ones that are sure to become favorites. This time, the setting takes place on a farm, where a group of teens are stuck together, learning more life lessons, and learning more about themselves. This installment is full of laughs, tears, heartfelt moments, and answers some questions left by *The Bench*.

The Lake: Living A Meaningful Life, is Book #3 in the "Living A Meaningful Life" series. In this, the most dramatic installment of the series yet, the main character is challenged like never before. After suffering what he feels is a devastating catastrophic blow to his future, he turns to his mentors who must inspire him to rise up from the ashes, and meet his full potential so that he may fulfill his destiny. *The Lake* will leave you truly inspired to face your own life challenges, and will help you realize that you CAN overcome anything if you believe in yourself and 'do the right things.' Prepare to laugh and cry along the way, and feel your soul renewed and inspired by the end of the book.

The Favor: Living A Meaningful Life, is Book #4 in the "Living A Meaningful Life" series. In this, the most pivotal and climactic installment of the series yet, the main character must make sacrifices for those who mean the most to him, as he faces life shattering losses, and must summon all of his strength, inner character, and utilize the life lessons taught to him by his mentors. He meets the moment for which his mentors have been preparing and grooming him for. This book has a particularly meaningful focus on dealing with grief from loss, especially when you find yourself alone in life after losing someone closest to you.

The Promise: Living A Meaningful Life, is Book #5 in the "Living A Meaningful Life" series. In this very emotional, inspiring, and touching installment of the series, the main character must once again make changes to his life in order to honor promises made. He realizes that sacrifices made, to honor promises given, can result in the greatest gifts that life has to offer. *The Promise* will stir within you deep emotions, and leave you contemplating your own life choices and possibilities. When we have the courage and discipline to 'do the right things,' for the right reasons, we are richly rewarded in ways that we cannot even imagine. There are plenty of tears in this one, but they are tears of joy. You will also enjoy an abundance of laughs, as you experience the banter between the characters we have come to know and love.

The Sacrifice: Living A Meaningful Life, is Book #6 in the "Living A Meaningful Life" series. In this very emotional, inspiring, and touching installment of the series, the main character and his family must once again 'do the right things,' and make huge sacrifices for the benefit of the community they love and swore to support. Huge sacrifices made, can result in huge blessings given. There are deeply moving ups and downs in this one, but you will enjoy an abundance of laughs, as you experience the banter between the characters we have come to know and love.

The Challenge: Living A Meaningful Life, is Book #7 in the "Living A Meaningful Life" series. In this very amusing, inspiring, and touching installment of the series, the young star of the series finally gets his chance to prove himself. He must endure trials and tribulations to see if he has what it takes to secure his place within the family dynasty. This is one of the high points of the series, and sets the direction for the next phase of the series. This installment is full of fun moments, and allows the reader to truly enjoy the teen who has become the favorite character of the series. You will enjoy an abundance of laughs, as you experience the banter between the characters we have come to know and love.

The Wedding: Living A Meaningful Life, is Book #8 in the "Living A Meaningful Life" series. In this very amusing and touching installment of the series, our favorite couple finally tie the knot. But that is by no means a spoiler, as there are some twists and turns involved. Our favorite young star does not disappoint in delivering to us more of his antics and genius. In one of the most hilarious moments in the series, there is a father/son discussion regarding our favorite teen "coming of age," and having his first girlfriend.

The Crew: Living A Meaningful Life, is Book #9 in the "Living A Meaningful Life" series. This very amusing, inspiring, and touching installment, gives us a closer look into Rudy's huge inner-circle of friends, and their hilarious antics. This installment is another high-point of the series, as it chronicles Rudy's growing success, but also features a very emotional event which rocks his world. How Rudy handles this "event" will prove him worthy of his destiny. This is a highly emotional installment, and will leave you changed as a person.

Surviving Life: Contemplations Of The Soul is a unique and powerful book full of compassion and empathy, which combines the issues of what hurts us the most, with thoughts and advice meant to empower us toward happiness and independence. **Surviving Life** is medicine for the soul. It guides us through our deepest pains and weaknesses, and leads us to a place of self-empowerment, inspiration, strength, and hope. The topics covered are raw, diverse, and very practical. **Surviving Life** includes many subjects, and answers many questions, such as, "What is your purpose on this planet," "When you think nobody loves you," "How can you feel good," as well as practical advice on battling depression, suicide, and figuring out who you truly are. **Surviving Life** is a practical and contemplative manual for people of all ages, and the perfect book for gifting to those who need guidance and love.

EVOLVE is a cutting-edge, unique, powerful, and practical personal transformation self-help improvement book, which examines human life and all of its issues from a unique futuristic approach with a touch of humor. A selection of topics include: healing from personal losses and traumas, coping with sadness and depression, moving past fear that others use to control, manipulate, and abuse you, clarity in thinking, advanced communication skills, evolving your relationships, exploring the meaning of life, how everything in the Universe is connected, developing your psychic ability, and a little discussion about aliens possibly living among us. Yes, there is everything, which is all directly tied back to your own personal life.

Heal Me is a powerful and touching book that will pull at your heartstrings, give you practical advice on overcoming a variety of life traumas, and will put you on the road to recovery and healing. *Heal Me* examines such issues as the death of a loved one, loss of a pet, suicide, anxiety, addiction, life failures, major life mistakes, broken relationships, abuse, sexual assault, self-esteem, living in a toxic world surrounded by toxic people, loneliness, and many other issues. This is a self-care book written in a very loving, practical, and informative way that you can gift to yourself, family, young people, and friends, as a gesture of love, support, and hope.

Rising To Greatness is a self-help book that takes you on a step-by-step transformation, from the ashes of being broken and lost, to the greatness of self-empowerment, accomplishment, and happiness. This book includes such topics as developing your sense of self, eliminating fear from your life, mastering your emotions, self-discipline and motivation, communication skills, and so much more.

LIVING A MEANINGFUL LIFE

BOOK SERIES INSTALLMENT SYNOPSIS

This is a series for adults, but has many themes, stories, and lessons, that would be enjoyed by a teen audience as well. Through its down-to-Earth, emotional, and touching storylines, the series shows the importance of developing self-empowerment, and a person's own deep character, through mentors, self-work, and 'soul-families.' The main theme is that of always 'doing the right things,' as a way of living a meaningful life. All installments within this series feature characters of all ages, from children to older adults. The series is neutral on religion and politics. There are tears of sadness, tears of joy, and lots of laughs. This is a series that changes lives.

Book #1, *The Bench*, is an important book that lays the foundation for the series. This installment provides the background for important mentors and characters featured in the series. This installment covers much of the main character's childhood, and provides important lessons learned, as well as a number of the back-stories referred to later on in the series.

Book #2, *The Farm*, is the more "juvenile" installment of the series, but is a critical book that provides the background on the most important mentor of the series, as well as many of the back-stories for the series. In this installment, the main character is a young teen. This is also a "coming of age" installment, where the main character realizes the meaning of leadership, and the importance of having a mentor.

Book #3, *The Lake*, is the installment where the main character transforms from a teenage child to a highly dynamic teenage young adult. This installment is a major turning-point in his life. His destiny is decided in this installment, but he doesn't know it yet.

Book #4, *The Favor*, is the most pivotal installment of the series. Everything changes, and the main character's future is laid out before him. Highly emotional and intense installment. The main character is now a young adult, and a new future star of the series is introduced.

Book #5, *The Promise*, is the 'relief' installment after the intensity of Book #4. The main character must accept his new life, and live up to his promises and obligations. The new rising star of the series begins to become very prominent.

Book #6, *The Sacrifice*, reminds us that things can always change in an instant. This installment tests the resolve of the main character, as he must draw upon the lessons taught to him by his mentors, as he faces his greatest challenge yet.

Book #7, *The Challenge*, is the next most pivotal installment, where the previously rising star of the series solidifies his prominence as THE star of the series. This installment exhibits the power that people can have if they dare to rise up and soar like an Eagle.

Book #8, *The Wedding,* gives us what we have been wanting and waiting for. But in addition to that, this is the "coming of age" installment for the young star of the series, who all of a sudden, blossoms into a young man with his own independence and ideas, as most older teenagers do. The young star continues to surpass all expectations.

Book #9, *The Crew*, gives us a closer look into Rudy's huge inner-circle of friends, and their antics. This installment is another high-point in the series, as it chronicles Rudy's growing success, but also a very emotional event which rocks his world. How Rudy handles this "event" will prove him worthy of his destiny. Highly emotional installment.

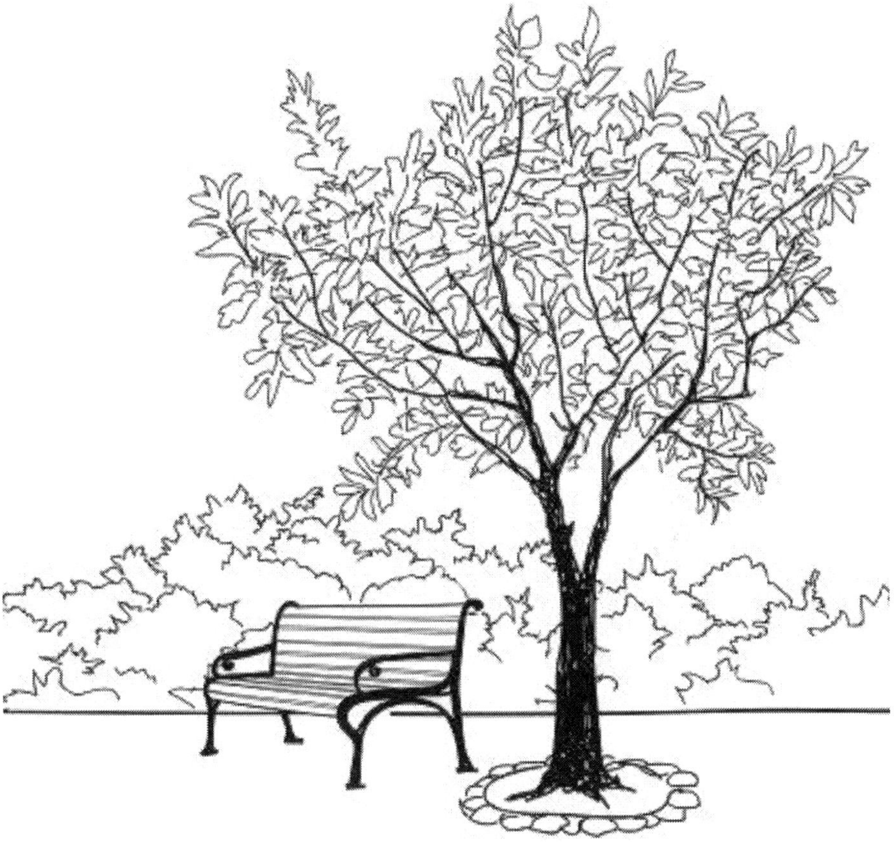

Printed in Great Britain
by Amazon